Praise for Alan Gelb's Approach

"Alan Gelb has done the impossible: he's created a sane and simple process for crafting a knock-your-socks-off essay! His guide is perfect for high school students facing the most important document they will ever write. The student still has to do the work, but Gelb's approach reduces the stress."

—**DONALD ASHER**, author of *Cool Colleges* and *Graduate Admissions Essays*

"Alan's guidance in the process of writing my college essay was invaluable. Not only did I end up with an immensely superior product than I would have without his help, I also learned, with Alan's help, how to mine the depths of my experience to find a meaningful narrative and then convey it with a clear, coherent structure. I got in early decision to Columbia University with that essay; I am forever indebted to Alan for that."

—**JOSH FREED**, admitted early decision to Columbia University

"Taking an ordinary essay and helping to mold it into an extraordinary one is what Alan Gelb does best. [He] helped transform ... my essay into a final draft that could stand out amongst an elite crowd."

—**MEGAN S. STEVEN, PhD**, one of Alan's first students, admitted to Dartmouth for undergrad and awarded a Rhodes Scholarship; now a faculty member with the Center for Cognitive Neuroscience, Dartmouth College

"Alan Gelb saved us by working with our daughters to help *them* understand what ... college ... daughters' admissions to Brown and ... by his advice."

—**JANE HIRSCH**

CONQUERING THE
COLLEGE
ADMISSIONS
ESSAY
IN 10 STEPS

CONQUERING THE
COLLEGE
ADMISSIONS
ESSAY
IN 10 STEPS

CRAFTING A WINNING
PERSONAL STATEMENT

THIRD EDITION

ALAN GELB

TEN SPEED PRESS
California | New York

Copyright © 2008, 2013, 2017 by Alan Gelb

Published in the United States by Ten Speed Press,
an imprint of the Crown Publishing Group, a division of
Penguin Random House LLC, New York.
www.crownpublishing.com
www.tenspeed.com

Ten Speed Press and the Ten Speed Press colophon are registered trademarks of
Penguin Random House, LLC

Earlier editions of this work were published in 2008 and 2013 in the United
States by Ten Speed Press, an imprint of the Crown Publishing Group, a division
of Penguin Random House LLC.

Library of Congress Cataloging-in-Publication Data
Names: Gelb, Alan, author.
Title: Conquering the college admissions essay in 10 easy steps : crafting a
winning personal statement / Alan Gelb.
Description: Third edition. | New York : Ten Speed Press, 2017. | Includes index.
Identifiers: LCCN 2016050125
Subjects: LCSH: College applications—United States. | Universities and
colleges—United States—Admission. | Exposition (Rhetoric) | Essay—
Authorship. | BISAC: STUDY AIDS / College Entrance. | EDUCATION /
Higher. | LANGUAGE ARTS & DISCIPLINES / Composition & Creative
Writing.
Classification: LCC LB2351.52.U6 G448 2017 | DDC 378.1/616—dc23
LC record available at https://lccn.loc.gov/2016050125

Trade Paperback ISBN: 978-0-399-57869-4
eBook ISBN: 978-0-399-57870-0

Printed in the United States of America

Design by Lizzie Allen

10 9 8 7 6 5 4 3 2 1

Third Edition

For Noah and Nathaniel, my sons and guinea pigs.

Contents

Acknowledgments

I deeply appreciate the interest of Ten Speed Press in publishing this book. I would like to thank Aaron Wehner, who first paid attention to it, and my subsequent editors, Melissa Moore, Emily Timberlake, Clara Sankey, and Ashley Pierce. Thank you as well to the students who allowed me to reprint their essays. I would also like to express my gratitude to all the students I have worked with over the years for allowing me to learn from them, and to my wife, Karen Levine, for always supporting me in my writing career.

Preface

I want to tell you a little bit about how I came to do this kind of work. I live in a small rural town in upstate New York where the high school is adequate—not more, sometimes less. Both of my sons aspired to go on to selective four-year colleges. They were good candidates—highly ranked in their classes, with excellent scores on their standardized tests and solid achievements that attested to their special talents. As I said, their high school offered them the basics but not much more. One "extra" that was not present was the kind of intense college preparation provided by exclusive private schools and affluent suburban high schools. When the time came to apply to college, kids around here were pretty much on their own.

Unlike my boys, I did not grow up in a small rural town. I went to high school in Scarsdale, New York—one of the most pressured public high schools in the country with one of the best college acceptance rates—and so I knew something about the process of getting into the school of one's choice. As a professional writer, I also knew how to craft an essay, so when the time came for my sons to work on their college applications, they were lucky to have an in-house coach.

My older son wrote an essay about growing up in a community where he felt "different"—he was one of only two Jewish kids in a graduating class of one hundred twenty—while my younger son wrote a piece about the burnout he had experienced as a competitive athlete. Both of my sons got into their first-choice colleges.

I soon found myself helping quite a few students in our town, and I enjoyed this contact. I got to know about them in personal and often very moving ways, and I had the satisfaction of seeing them learn some valuable lessons about writing. As the years went by, and as I worked with more and more students, I realized that my approach to this assignment was quite original in its attention to the narrative form, and so I decided to collect my theories in the book you're about to read.

Since its original publication, I have coached many more students, all over the world, and I have blogged and lectured widely on the subject of the college admissions essay. Many teachers have told me that they use this book in their classroom, so I have created a teacher's guide (see page 222) to make the book even more teacher-friendly. It has been exciting to see my book appear in a second edition and now I am even more excited about this third edition, which proves that revision is an absolutely critical part of the writing process, something we'll be talking about a lot more as we go on. This time around I've also ventured more substantively into the subject of supplemental essays, a very important and oftentimes confounding part of the admissions process.

Since this book was first published in 2008, a great many of my readers have told me how useful it has been to them, and that is very gratifying. I hope that you too will learn valuable lessons as you read and digest this book and that you will come away with an original, authentic personal statement. You will also gain some insights into how to write strong supporting essays on your academic goals and objectives, your most significant extra-curricular activities, and more. We will even touch on the increasingly important letters that you may want to write in response to being placed on a wait list. All of these writings come together to help the admissions committee form an impression of you in ways that the rest of your admissions packet cannot convey.

Introduction

If you're looking for an instruction book on how to write the college application essay, you'll be happy to know that there are quite a few excellent ones on the market. In fact, if you have all the time in the world, I suggest you check out as many of these as you can. Chances are, they'll all contain some useful ideas. But if you're pressed for time—and what high school senior isn't?—then you can feel confident that the book at hand is your fastest and surest way to produce the kind of application essay you're after.

How is this book different from all the others out there? First of all, it has been pared down to the essentials. I've coached a great many students through this process and know that it doesn't make any sense to choose the first semester of the senior year as the time to "share secrets from college admissions counselors" or "sample essays from great writers like E. B. White, George Orwell, and Oliver Wendell Holmes." This is the time when you want to focus exclusively on that which is absolutely critical, eliminate anything that feels like padding, and simply get the job done in the best possible way as fast as you can.

To that end, I've organized this learning process into a ten-step system. I'd like to say ten "easy" steps because "easy" is such a persuasive word, like "new," "improved," and "best ever." But the truth is that some of these steps are not that "easy." That said, none is insurmountable. If you follow this book in its logical sequence, you will arrive at your destination—a well-turned college application essay designed to linger in the minds of those who read it.

My book is different from others on this subject in that it focuses entirely on process. As I said, I will not be offering any extraneous material, like "secrets" from admissions counselors at Harvard, Princeton, or Yale. Such secrets are enticing, but ultimately do little to help your cause. What will help is to truly understand the elements of a well-constructed narrative, which is what this book will be teaching.

THE RULES OF THE GAME

I always begin my work with students by laying out two cardinal rules. Rule #1 is that students must have complete ownership over their essays. No one is going to write it for them. Regrettably, there are essay services out there that actually *do* the writing for students, or at least the lion's share of the job. Not only is this practice highly unethical, but it is also profoundly wrongheaded. No one can write a personal essay for you that will be nearly as effective as the one you write for yourself. So if anyone offers to do such a thing—your mother, father, sister, brother, or, heaven forbid, a hired gun—*just say no*. Your essay needs to present your authentic voice.

Rule #2 is very clear: it simply states that you have to work at the process. When I'm coaching a student on the college essay, I act more like an editor than a teacher. At various points in my life, I've been a teacher and at other times an editor, and I know you can be a teacher who edits and an editor who teaches. These two vocations, however, embrace somewhat different objectives when it comes to writing. As a teacher, it is my inclination to allow students to travel at their own speed toward their place of discovery. I can suggest that they make a turn up ahead or go back a few blocks, but they're driving the car. On the other hand, as an editor I appreciate the need to get to a certain place by a certain time—"the deadline."

As a high school senior, you know all about deadlines. You know when your college application is due, and so, with that understanding, the basis for Rule #2 becomes so much clearer: you have to work hard at the process in order to achieve your product. You have to stay with it, even when you're feeling like you'll never get it right, and the more focused you become, the better your chances for success will be.

Now even though I'm bringing an editorial perspective to this job, I'm sorry to say I might not actually get to *be* your editor. Over the years, as I would help students with their essays, I came to realize that I have a special understanding of this task and a special talent for helping people turn out their best work. In fact, I discovered that I was so good at it that I decided to turn my coaching service into a sideline business. I now act as an editor for students who hire me—never as a writer. That would violate Rule #1—the rule about ownership—which will remain for now and always inviolable. I won't kid you—it's useful to have me on hand to help with an essay. But that's a luxury, and, since I may not be available to you on a one-to-one basis, I'm going to teach you how to be your *own* editor. By focusing on process, *Conquering the College Admissions Essay in 10 Steps* will function as a crash course in self-editing—a skill you can use now, as you perfect your college application essay, and in the future, for all of your writing assignments.

Why is the essay so important in today's college application process? Let's think about it. Back in the old days when I applied to college, there was something called The Interview. You, the student, put on a professional outfit and a polished pair of shoes and you sat down in a wood-paneled room with someone from the school who asked you weighty questions. Or perhaps you suffered through an "alumni interview," answering questions put to you by some portly banker or physician who reminded you of that great-uncle you saw only at family functions. Either way, it wasn't a whole lot of fun.

Today, the interview has pretty much gone the way of yesteryear's gas fill-up where you had your windows washed and your oil level checked. Maintaining an admissions staff that conducts on-campus interviews is just too costly for most schools. These days, college admissions personnel are on the road most of the time, out recruiting students. So, if a college or university should happen to offer interviews, they do so mostly for informational purposes—to inform *you*, not to inform themselves *about* you. What's more, these interviews are often conducted by graduate students or even undergrads who are looking to pick up pin money and whose assessments may not count for very much. Your essay, in essence, *is* your "interview." It's your chance to shine in the eyes of the admissions officer who reads it. He or she will form some kind of opinion of you as a person and as a writer, and that opinion may determine which stack your application lands on.

The essay has become one of the most important parts of the entire application process. A recent survey from the National Association for College Admission Counseling ranked the essay as the fifth most significant determinant in getting into college—after grades in college preparatory classes, the strength of a student's curriculum, admission test scores, and grades in all other courses, but ahead of recommendations, class rank, and extracurricular activities. Perhaps even more significantly, these admissions counselors named the essay as the single most important "tip factor"—that is, the thing that can tip your application in your favor, all other factors being equal.

It makes sense if you think about it. When you apply to a selective college or university, you'll be competing against many other students who have terrific grades and exemplary scores on their standardized tests. That's a given. Every one of you will have secured glowing recommendations from your teachers. You're all going to have a laundry list of extracurricular activities and honors and awards and so forth. Now, of course, there are some extraordinarily gifted students who have perfect SATs and straight A averages, who have managed to isolate hitherto unknown hormones while achieving national ranking in two sports, and who have rescued people from floodwaters when they weren't singing *lieder* in recitals at symphony halls. Those students could write essays about how to boil turnips and they'd get into the school of their choice.

For the rest of you, the essay really can serve as the tip factor—the one part of the packet that you can make totally your own, unique and memorable. In a sense, it's your thumbprint. No two essays are alike, after all. The point is that you have the chance to write an essay that will serve as the perfect expression of who you are and how you function in the world. You can captivate and astound your audience; reduce bored, jaded readers to tears; and make them want to meet you the moment you arrive on campus in the fall. (A number of students I have worked with have reported back to me that when they arrived on campus at the beginning of their first year, an admissions counselor rushed over to ask whether they wrote *that* essay.) What an opportunity this essay is, when you think about it. But that's just the problem for so many students—thinking about it.

It's perfectly normal when faced with such an important task to freeze. The problem is compounded by the fact that the essay is usually dealt with toward the end of the college application process, when students and parents are exhausted. And if that weren't enough to keep you from writing, there's also the fact that when most people sit down to write *anything*, a certain degree of resistance is bound to kick in. Overcoming resistance to writing is, in fact, an ongoing problem that even professional writers have to conquer over and over again. To tell you the truth, when I sat down to start this book, I experienced so much resistance that I indulged in every possible distraction, like cleaning, cooking, talking on the phone, and compulsively checking my email. I finally removed myself to a nearby library where I knew I wouldn't be distracted.

In short, the work is hard and there's a lot at stake. That's enough to make anyone freeze. Keep in mind, however, that there are many great colleges out there. If you don't get into an Ivy, you will survive. If you don't get into your first choice, or your second, or your third, you will survive. You will get into your fourth or fifth choice, and you will do just fine in life. But at least now, as you're striving toward whatever goal you've established for yourself, you'll know that one part of your job—writing your essay—is something you definitely *can* accomplish, and it is my firm belief that you can accomplish it in three drafts and a polish. So there— I've thrown down the gauntlet. Let's get started, shall we?

Understanding the Narrative

Gather around while I tell you a story:

> Jessie went to the store.

Wow. That was some story, wasn't it? No? Didn't quite do it for you? All right. Let's try again.

> Jessie went to the store. She bought bread, butter, cheese, sardines, lemonade, air freshener, panty hose, dog treats, peanut butter, and Crisco.

Better? No? Boy—tough room. Okay, I'll keep trying.

> Jessie went to the store. She bought bread, butter, cheese, sardines, lemonade, air freshener, panty hose, dog treats, peanut butter, and Crisco. As she headed toward the car, her shopping bag broke.

Ahhh. Now we're cooking. Much better, no? But what happened to make it better? The answer is *something*. Something happened. The bag broke, conflict reared its head, and the story started to come alive.

From the moment that Jessie's bag breaks, anything can happen. A tall, dark stranger could come over to help. As they gather up her cans and cartons, their eyes meet. They wind up in a diner. Jessie discovers that the stranger is a political refugee from Iran, looking for somewhere to hide.

If you're not particularly moved by that plotline, let's go in a whole other direction. Maybe Jessie bends down, and, as she retrieves the jar of peanut butter, something bright and gleaming catches her eye. There, on the sidewalk, is a heart-shaped locket. Inside the locket is a letter that a Civil War soldier sent to his bride. And so we have a story within a story. Interesting. . . .

Or maybe the plastic egg holding the panty hose rolls down the sidewalk and falls through the sewer grate. Jessie reaches in to scoop it out and . . . her hand gets stuck! The entire neighborhood—men, women, children, police, firefighters, and assorted SWAT teams—descends in a raucous free-for-all. Suddenly, we have a comedy on our hands.

In each of these instances, the inciting action is the same—the shopping bag breaks—but in each case, it sparks entirely different currents of conflict. As a writer, you decide which direction to send your story in. Do you want romance? Mystery? Comedy? Or perhaps you'd prefer to head in the direction of a subtler internal drama. Maybe Jessie is tired of being the unloved child in an abusive family. Maybe the broken bag and the prospect of parental disapproval is the last straw that somehow gets her to hop on a bus and go in search of a new life. As you see, writing is all about choices.

Making Choices

Writing is sometimes compared to sculpting. You start out with an inert mass—words instead of clay—and, as you shape and mold it, hopefully some measure of form, feeling, and movement will emerge. Another way to look at writing is that it's like making a sauce—you start with raw ingredients, which you then cook down until you've made something very concentrated and flavorful.

As a writer, you have to be completely ruthless about what works and what doesn't. A well-known, if macabre, adage is that writing is "all about killing your babies." The point is that no matter how much you might love a particular sentence or hold an image dear to your heart, if it doesn't serve the overall purpose of the piece, then it has no business being there.

But before we start to worry about sentences or words or images, or even about our choice of subject, we have to come to a real understanding of the narrative form. The form of your essay—dictated to a large extent by the word allotment you'll be working with—precludes your rendering the *entire* trip you took last summer to Yosemite National Park or your *entire* season playing lacrosse for Indian Head High School. The point right now is to forget about your subject and concentrate on learning and understanding the narrative form.

A Narrative Is . . .

When you're narrating, you're telling a story. The story is a sequence of events. It may be a long story—*The Odyssey, The Adventures of Huckleberry Finn, Lord of the Rings*—or it could be as short as a joke. The story can be real or it can be fictional. It can have a cast of characters or it can all take place inside one person's head.

When you narrate, the first problem you have to handle is time. As I said before, you're not going to have enough time or space to deal with your entire trip to Yosemite National Park. And—no offense—there are few people, aside from your grandparents, who would be interested in hearing about your entire trip. So you're going to have to choose one aspect of your trip, and one of the ways you'll choose is by deciding what you feel you can most effectively convey in the limited amount of space (time) you have to work with. The other way you'll choose is by deciding which aspect of your trip offers the best solutions to the other narrative problems we'll be talking about in this chapter:

1. "The Once"
2. The Ordinary vs. The Extraordinary
3. Tension and Conflict
4. The Point

But more about those later. For now, let's think about what makes a good storyteller.

Consider all the people you know. Think about your Uncle Saul, for instance—he tells a heck of a story, doesn't he? That one about the time he was running with the bulls in Pamplona and had to jump over a bridge into the river to escape the marauding beasts? That's a great story, even though you've heard it every Thanksgiving since you were knee-high. But Uncle Saul knows *how* to tell a story. He offers vivid details—looking back over his shoulder to see the snot of the bull flying through the air, and the sound of the bull's hooves clattering on the narrow cobblestone streets—but, even more than the details, he knows just when and where to pick up the story and is able to establish a rhythm that rushes you along to its thrilling conclusion. There is a wonderful kind of *whoosh* to the story—like riding a raft down a chute at a water park. And, because Uncle Saul has told his story so many times, he has cooked it down to its finest essence. There are no unnecessary details. No ruffles or flourishes to slow things down. Even though you've heard it so many times, you still tingle with excitement as the bull gains on him and he vaults over the side of the bridge.

Now think of someone you know who has no idea how to tell a story, or even a joke. Like—your mother. Now, you love your mother. She's great. She's cool. She doesn't get on you for all the things most mothers do, and she's a really good cook and can even beat you at a 5K race every now and then. Yep—there's a lot to recommend Mom. But one thing she does not know how to do is tell a story. Here she is with a story that starts in one place—in the Bed and Bath department at Macy's—and you think it's going to be all about buying towels (should she have chosen lilac or pink, bath sheets or regular bath towels, or maybe she should've waited for a sale altogether), and then who should she run into but Marjorie Wills, Jackie Wills's mom, who told her that Jackie was going to be a lifeguard this summer at Candlestick Lake, but then Jackie's always been such a good swimmer (uh, Mom, I've got homework to do), and then, as she was leaving the store, she realized that she left her purse on the counter. She ran back and . . . there it was! And then, on the way out, she saw that the blenders were on sale, and ever since Dad dropped a bottle cap into their blender it hasn't sounded quite right—

That's the story, Mom?

Yes, honey, that's the story. I sure was lucky, wasn't I?

As it turned out, not only was Mom's story virtually without conflict—except for the two minutes where she thought she might have lost her purse—but it was also filled with extraneous details (Jackie the excellent swimmer, the lilac and pink towels, and so on). Worst of all, it didn't know where to start or where to end. Mom's handling of time in this narrative was . . . well, it was just plain *bad*.

What a Narrative Needs

For a narrative to function as it should, it has to address certain basic problems. All readers come to what they're reading with expectations—that they're not going to be bored and that they're going to understand why they bothered to read this thing in the first place—and those expectations must be met. The most immediate problem that the writer has to figure out in order to meet the reader's expectations is how to handle time. Let's call that "The Once."

"THE ONCE"

"The Once" is that specific point in time in which the narrative is situated—like "once upon a time," that traditional opening for fairy tales. One of the most dramatic examples I can think of when it comes to managing time is Ray Bradbury's classic story "All Summer in a Day." This nine-hundred-thirty-eight-word narrative, set on a distant planet where the sun appears for only one day a year, follows a central character, a victimized child named Margot, who is locked into a closet by bullies on that one day of the sun's appearance and misses the whole thing. "The Once" in this incredibly gripping, extremely short story is wondrously compressed, so you are right there, beside Margot, as you experience her anguish every agonizing step of the way.

Now, let's look back at Mom's story to see how she mishandled "The Once." There was no good reason why Mom had to start her story way back where she did. Yes, it's a fact that she was choosing between bath sheets and bath towels, but, in terms of the story, it wasn't a fact that the reader had to be bothered with. We didn't need to run into Marjorie Wills either, or to learn that Jackie Wills was working as a lifeguard for the summer. The story, such as it was (and, as we concluded, it wasn't much), kicked in, if only momentarily, when Mom lost the purse. Suddenly, there was some conflict. (Just remember the term *conflict*, because we're going to be returning to the subject in a moment.) In the story fragment at the beginning of this chapter about Jessie, the girl who went grocery shopping, you'll recall that the conflict was introduced when Jessie's bag broke, thereby igniting the action of the story. In Mom's story, the conflict came when she forgot her purse. This was meant to set off the action, but, unfortunately, Mom was unable to construct a narrative that could carry that action along.

Now let's assume for the moment that there actually was a real, good story that Mom could have made out of that forgotten purse. What might that story have been about? Well, here's an idea—it could have been about a woman who feels dissatisfied with her role as homemaker. She's out shopping for towels, and perhaps she's feeling regretful about not having achieved the exciting, dramatic life she'd always hoped she'd have. As she's rummaging through the towels, feeling the soft terry, she thinks back to herself as a young woman—a promising swimmer who, if she had really applied herself, might have made it to the Olympics. She pictures herself toweling down at the side of the pool, ready and eager for adventure and success. As she pays for the towels, she's still adrift in that sea of wistful memories, and it isn't until she gets to the car that she realizes she's left her purse behind. Rushing back to Macy's, she experiences a startling moment of self-discovery. She realizes that she's put herself at risk—not just literally, by forgetting her purse, but existentially, by losing herself in memories that undercut her life as a wife and mother. When she finds that the purse is just where she left it, she takes that as a gift—and a sign—that she should value what she has. And that's why she's ultimately drawn to the blenders on sale, because, once again, she's back into her role as wife and mother. She's resolved her conflict, at least for now.

Okay, this may not be a story that races your motor, but it is a story that could be gracefully, purposefully, and dramatically told, one in which all the problems of a narrative could be successfully solved.

THE ORDINARY VS. THE EXTRAORDINARY

Another basic problem that a writer must address when constructing a narrative is to figure out the "extraordinary" thing that's going on in it. A story deserves to be told when something out of the ordinary is happening. The story of Jessie, back at the beginning of this chapter, did not deserve to be told if all we were going to be hearing about were her sardines, her air freshener, and her panty hose. That was utterly ordinary stuff and unworthy of anyone's attention. But when Jessie's bag broke, the *extraordinary* occurred, and the story (or, at least, the potential story) began to unfold.

It's the same with Mom's story. There was all that excruciatingly ordinary stuff about the towels and running into Marjorie Wills and what have you, and then there was the *extraordinary* (or, at least, the "out of the ordinary") event of the purse being left behind. We should note too that forgetting or potentially losing one's purse is an event that holds even more potential for the extraordinary—like losing one's money, one's identity, one's equilibrium, and so on.

TENSION AND CONFLICT

When we hear or read a narrative, we look to see how the extraordinary event works toward resolving the Tension and Conflict that act as a kind of frame for the piece. If we think in terms of multiple dimensions, the time sequence of the narrative—whether it be a picnic, a raft ride, an intimate conversation, a gymnastics performance, a walk with your dog, or a hundred other "pieces of time"—is one kind of frame. Superimposed on top of this frame is the Tension and Conflict frame. While leaving a purse at a store counter may be *extraordinary* (in the sense of being "out of the ordinary"), it is not in and of itself very interesting unless the writer places it within the context of some kind of conflict.

What does forgetting the purse signify? I've suggested that a story could be written about a homemaker's conflict regarding her role and how it would play itself out through a moment of negligence. In the scenarios proposed for the story of Jessie and her broken shopping bag, I suggested that one possibility might be that the broken bag would serve as the catalyst for her meeting a mysterious stranger and possibly getting involved in some international intrigue. The conflict in that particular story choice might be that Jessie is a small-town innocent, unwise to the ways of the world and susceptible to manipulation, and the tension comes from finding out whether and how she's going to get trapped in something that could prove to be very dangerous.

By the time you've reached the end of the narrative—whether you're writing it or reading it—you should have the answer to the question, why? That's the question that lies at the foundation of any and all narratives. Why am I reading this? Why should I bother? What am I going to get out of it? What's the point of it all?

Sometimes The Point of a narrative is made absolutely explicit, as in Aesop's fables, for instance. Whether the fables are about milkmaids or crows, foxes or hares, The Point (or moral) is clearly stated at the end. Now look at the story of the woman who leaves her purse at the counter and try to figure out what its point might be. How about, Never take what you have for granted? That would work, wouldn't it? As for the story of Jessie and the broken bag, no matter which direction you choose to go in, there's a point to be made. Whether the broken bag serves as the catalyzing event that initiates the international intrigue (keep your eyes open and watch your back), or leads to the discovery of the Civil War locket (you never know what treasures lurk at your feet), or results in Jessie's neighbors freeing her hand from the sewer grate (always depend on the kindness of strangers), your story will only become a fulfilling reading experience when its point is made evident.

Ultimately, we may decide that none of these points is interesting enough to justify the stories, but at least each one has some potential. And remember—a point doesn't have to jump out at you and shake you by the hand. Don't get the idea that I'm urging you to state any of these points as I've stated them above. After all, you're not Aesop. The Point of a narrative can be very subtle, even elusive. Some of the best narratives require that you spend a few moments thinking about what it is that you've just read and what, in fact, The Point might be.

Conflict Is . . .

I've been using the term *conflict* all along, but now I'd like to explain what it really means. Conflict is the struggle between opposing forces, with the reader waiting to see whether and how the conflict can be resolved. Conflicts can exist between individual characters (Luke Skywalker and Darth Vader in *Star Wars*), between groups of characters (the Montagues and the Capulets in *Romeo and Juliet*), between individuals and society (Guy Montag and the futuristic book-burning culture in *Fahrenheit 451*), between individuals and nature (*Robinson Crusoe*), or between individuals and their own demons (*Dr. Jekyll and Mr. Hyde*). Conflicts can be supremely easy to identify and figure out, as in fairy tales—Hansel and Gretel vs. the Witch, the Three Little Pigs vs. the Wolf—or they can be quite complicated, often with a central character who is not even aware of his or her conflict until it's too late (Jay Gatsby in *The Great Gatsby*).

Classical storytelling is characterized by certain consistent elements. Among these are a protagonist who is active, who deals with external conflict in continuous time and reality, and who, at the end, finds a neatly wrapped (though sometimes tragic) resolution. Hercules, Pocahontas, and Robin Hood are all examples of classical heroes.

Modern heroes operate differently. Here the emphasis is often on internal conflict, sometimes with a passive protagonist who exists within an antistructure where the time and reality are not continuous or consistent and where things are not neatly wrapped up at the end. Yossarian in Joseph Heller's *Catch-22*, Alex in *A Clockwork Orange*, and Holden Caulfield in J. D. Salinger's *The Catcher in the Rye* are good examples of the modern hero.

In the narrative that you'll be writing for your college application, you may be more successful working with a classical structure than with a modern structure, even if you feel more like a modern hero (which, I suspect, you do). The point is that you'll want to have a fairly clear line from conflict to resolution. After all, you have only some six hundred fifty words to work with. You may also want to come across as a person who can identify a problem and solve it—an active person with good ideas, energy, resolve, and courage. This essay, after all, is your place to shine, not to let all your "modern" neuroses hang out.

Making a Story

In our next chapter, we'll explore conflict and resolution further, when we discuss topics to write about. For now, however, I'd like to show you what I came up with for an essay that uses the "broken shopping bag" as a springboard. See whether you think I've created a narrative that solves all the problems we've been exploring in this chapter.

Sardines, lemonade, dog treats . . .

This was my summer—bagging groceries at Uncle Wiggly's, with no possibility of escape.

"Careful of the Velveeta," the old lady said.

. . . peanut butter, panty hose, Crisco . . .

"And watch out for the English muffins."

"Can I help you to the car, ma'am?"

"No, thank you. Do I look like I need help?" she said, taking up her bag and heading toward the parking lot.

All my friends were doing interesting things this summer. Going to Europe to play tennis. Building houses in Guatemala. Interning in New York City. And here I was, getting paid minimum wage and spending my days alongside cashiers like Flo, a biker chick with tattoos up and down her arms, and Jerod, who used to be in advertising until his firm went under, not to mention Corey, the bag boy at the next station who had Down syndrome. How would I spin this one on my college application? I wondered. "Interned in Bag Technology"? "Discovered Method to Protect Velveeta from Heavy Objects"?

"Dave!" I heard Mr. Simon, the manager, call from his post. "A lady in the parking lot needs help!"

I looked up. The old lady we had just checked out was standing in the middle of cans, jars, and, yes, Velveeta. The bag had broken, scattering her stuff everywhere. If she took a step, she might trip on something and break a hip. I grabbed a handful of bags and rushed outside.

"Careful, ma'am," I called. "Just stay where you are."

"You should've double-bagged it," she said.

I'm in big trouble, I thought as I bent down to collect the items. I hadn't paid attention. I was too busy thinking about what was wrong with my job to do it right. Now she was going to make a stink and then I'd be out of a job altogether, with even less to write about on my college application.

"There," I said. "I got it all."

As I walked toward her car, she was shaking her head. "You should've double-bagged it," she said again.

"I know. I'm sorry."

"I could've hurt myself."

"I'm really, really sorry."

She stared at me as I carefully placed the bag in her trunk. "Oh, well," she said. "Everyone makes mistakes. That's how you learn."

I stood there, in total amazement, as she reached into her bag and pulled out a dime.

"Here," she said, handing it to me.

"Thanks," I managed to say.

As I headed back inside, I realized that I had learned two valuable lessons that day—not to judge people and not to denigrate work. No matter what your job is, there's a right way and a wrong way to do it. I could learn from the old lady, I could learn from Flo, Jerod, and Corey, and I could learn from Uncle Wiggly.

I put the dime in my shirt pocket, where it would be safe. I resolved never to spend it. Those ten cents meant a lot to me.

So there you have it—a very solid college application essay. I had approached this task as a challenge: Could there be an interesting essay in a broken supermarket bag? I realized immediately that it would have to be told from the first person point of view. Almost inevitably, you'll be using first-person for your essay as well (more about point of view as we go along). So then, if I was going to tell this in the first person, who was the narrator going to be? How about a young man working in an Uncle Wiggly supermarket for the summer?

The second sentence sets up the conflict: the young man is stuck in a job he doesn't like, "with no possibility of escape." The tension around the conflict is carried along as we read on. His friends are all in enviable situations in glamorous places like Europe and New York, while he's stuck in a rut, surrounded by people he views as losers. So right away, as we can see, the narrative is addressing the Tension and Conflict problem.

How does it handle the problem of time (that is, "The Once")? Well, for one thing, it's quite compressed. And it starts right in the middle of things. Starting *in medias res* can be a very effective technique when you're dealing with such a short piece. Indeed, the entire scope of the action probably covers five minutes at most.

With the brief amount of space you're allotted for your essay, it can be useful—*but not obligatory*—to restrict yourself to an event that only occupies a brief amount of time.

What about The Ordinary vs. The Extraordinary? Yes, that's here too, represented by the catalyzing event we've been talking about all through this chapter—the breaking of the shopping bag. This is the *extraordinary* event that turns the story around and sends the reader in an interesting direction. As a final bonus, the story has another extraordinary event—the dime tip—that sends it in yet another direction.

And, finally, we get The Point, which is stated explicitly in this piece. The main character has learned some valuable lessons. He will keep the dime—the paltry tip that has become the unlikely symbol of his transformation. If you recall what we talked about in the introduction—how the essay is, in a sense, your "interview" and your opportunity to shine as a writer and as a person—you'll see that in this essay, that opportunity has been seized. In the course of 498 words, the writer presents himself as someone who has undergone significant growth, moving from a callow, bored youth to a more mature person of substance. He's gone from being dismissive of his coworkers to realizing that he can learn from them. He's internalized two critically important lessons: not to judge other people too quickly and never to discount the work you do. And he's shown the readers on the admissions panel that he has an ironic sense of humor (the Velveeta). The writer has accomplished a lot in the space allotted.

Now this essay took me all of ten minutes to write. I'm not bragging—I'm a professional writer who is not fazed by the prospect of making choices. At the moment, I like this essay. By tomorrow, I may like it less. I may find parts of it too pat or facile.

I may decide that the whole thing doesn't fall together well. I may give it to someone whose opinion I value, and that person may tell me it just doesn't work. We'll spend an ample amount of time in this book on feedback and self-editing, but it's important to know right at the beginning that everything looks different the next day and, more often than not, it doesn't look as good. What I can honestly say, however, is that this essay shows an understanding of the narrative form and, while it may not be brilliant, it does meet the two basic expectations of the reader: it is not boring (that is to say, something "extraordinary" occurs) and it makes a clearly identifiable point. (Also important to note: To my mind, this essay shows that you can write a perfectly good college essay about a summer job, whether it's bagging groceries, washing cars, being a lifeguard, or babysitting, and you don't have to go on some trip your family can ill afford to build houses in Haiti, or tutor kids in Thailand, or work at an unpaid internship in a glamor industry. Don't buy into that.)

Recap

1. Writing is all about making choices.

2. Writers have to solve four problems when they write a narrative: "The Once," The Ordinary vs. The Extraordinary, Tension and Conflict, and The Point.

3. "The Once" has to do with figuring out how to situate a narrative in time.

4. The Extraordinary is the unusual event that triggers the action.

5. Tension and Conflict create a context in which the story is told.

6. Conflict can occur between individuals, between groups, between an individual and society, between an individual and nature, and between an individual and his or her own private demons.

7. The Point makes it clear why the reader should have bothered to spend time with the narrative altogether.

Finding Your Topic

Far and away, the question I'm asked most often by students is, "What should I write about?" That's a big question indeed, and it certainly doesn't pertain only to student writers. All writers ask themselves that question. Finding a topic that can fully engage your interest as well as your reader's is never an easy thing, but once it comes to you, your essay should begin to flow—or at least trickle in a meaningful way. In this chapter, I'll provide you with strategies for uncovering workable topics and for getting started with this assignment that's been looming so large.

But first let's take a moment to review your task. The goal of your college essay—like the goal of any piece of writing—is to capture the attention and interest of your reader. When you sit down to write your essay, I want you to think about that reader who has been buried beneath an avalanche of "personal statements," many of which are numbing at best and wholly misconceived at worst. Why do college essays so often miss the mark? Here are some of the reasons:

- **They are utterly predictable.** They approach the assignment in the most formulaic way and emerge with a product that is, for the most part, a banal variation on a familiar theme.
- **They are sentimental to the point of being maudlin.** They seek to impress the reader not with the power of the writing but with the presumed pathos of a leg fractured during football season or a pet that has died prematurely. (Not that you can't write powerfully about those topics; you just shouldn't rely on the pathos, as if those stories can tell themselves.)
- **They are ineptly told.** They start here, wander there, and ultimately wind up nowhere.
- **They are shamelessly self-promoting.** They are less interested in telling a tale than in noting the writer's achievements. Look at me, they shout—I'm a junior emergency medical technician, an inner city tutor, a concert pianist, or some other form of shining wonder.

The college essay is not the place to tout one's achievements as much as it is a place to explore one's feelings about the world and how one fits into it. If you want the colleges to know about your impressive achievements, don't worry—that information will find its way into your application. In fact, I often tell students that a strong personal statement should essentially do three things: (1) show that you are a likable, sincere, self-reflective person who can help make up a college community; (2) show some arc of development so that the reader knows you better by the time he or she has finished reading your essay; and (3) show that you are a proficient writer. If you just do those three things, you should be in quite good shape with this assignment.

Getting Started

Confronting a blank piece of paper at the beginning of a writing session is one of life's genuine horrors. Douglas Adams, author of the classic comic novel *The Hitchhiker's Guide to the Galaxy*, captured the agony perfectly when he said, "Writing is easy. You only need to stare at a piece of paper until your forehead bleeds."

This "staring" part of the writing process cannot be avoided, and don't let anyone tell you otherwise. Like it or not, you're going to have to put in that staring time, and, when you're not staring, chances are you'll be walking around in circles, bouncing a ball against the wall, or closing your eyes and drifting off to sleep. Your mind and body conspire in all sorts of ways to distract you from the tough business at hand, but your spirit and your desire to succeed will hopefully hold you to your task. The horror will pass, and the words will come.

I've been a professional writer all of my adult life, and I still go through some version of the above whenever I sit down to write. I suddenly find something in my office that urgently needs cleaning—like the walls—and I'll distract myself for as long as it takes until my self-discipline asserts itself. (It always does. I write for a living, and looking at a stack of bills is an excellent motivator.) Allow time for your self-discipline to kick in. If you're staring or doodling, or even if you're just rolled up into a ball, and your mother or father starts bugging you to "get that essay done," just say that you're working on it, because, in fact, you are. You're doing the hardest part: confronting and overcoming the fear. Fortunately, just as my need to make a living acts as a strong external motivator, so does your college application deadline. Whether your deadline is in November, December, or January, you know that your time will come and you can't afford to be a day late. Your application must be sent in when it's due, and it must include a complete and polished essay.

Let me alert you to a critical reality: you're *not* going to be able to produce your best essay in a matter of twenty-four hours. Not in forty-eight hours. Doubtful in seventy-two. Not that it's impossible—I'll grant you that—but I'm a writer with a lot of experience and I wouldn't want to raise the stakes that high. I have to be able to sit with a piece of writing for a period of time in order to produce my best work. What may look good on Monday inevitably fails to pass muster on Tuesday and can seem utterly without merit on Wednesday. Give yourself the time you need— the time that any and all writers need—and don't try to rush that which is not meant to be rushed. Not only will you want to mull over what you've written, but you'll also want to allow time to get readings from other people.

So there you are, looking for something to write about, feeling fairly freaked out by all the pressure, and with that hateful piece of paper—or, more likely, computer screen—staring back at you. You've walked in circles, you've bounced your ball, you've checked your phone five or ten times, and now you have to settle down to work. Your next step should be some creative brainstorming.

As a general rule, I'm not much drawn to the term *brainstorming*. To me, it has the ring of educational jargon. But since you're probably familiar with the term, we can use it as a frame of reference. Essentially, brainstorming and mind-mapping are ways to prod your mind into a thinking mode. And that's what you're going to be doing as you approach this assignment—some very concentrated thinking.

A good way to ignite your thinking is to consider the various reasons why people write in the first place. Here are some reasons that come to my mind:

- To connect with other people
- To come to terms with something in the past
- To project into the future
- To better understand something in nature
- To amuse
- To arouse
- To preserve a tradition or folkway
- To explore a value or reinforce a moral standard
- To alarm a reader or otherwise provide a cautionary tale
- To confess
- To forgive

There are other reasons as well—probably you can think of some to add. In any case, if you look back at this list once you've completed your essay, you'll probably discover that what you've written consciously or unconsciously addresses one of those reasons above. And your impulse in writing—whether it is to confess, to forgive, to amuse, or to arouse—will be strongly connected to the *why* of your narrative, which we discussed in Step One.

Another way I begin to help students uncover a workable essay topic is by pointing out two main objectives. Objective #1 is to choose a topic that will present the writer in a good light. After all, this is your occasion to shine. Not to be a shining wonder, but to shine in the sense of distinguishing yourself as a *real* human being and establishing yourself as someone who will contribute something to a college community, as I said earlier. Putting forth your reality in a memorable way is a big part of this essay-writing task. You want to be seen as sympathetic, thoughtful, and, above all, honest. Not necessarily warts-and-all honest—you don't want to display your hang-ups in a way that might actually scare off an admissions counselor—but honest in the sense that you acknowledge your fallibility and affirm your openness to learning through experience.

Objective #2 involves selecting a topic that you can write about effectively, according to the outline of the narrative laid out in Step One. One of those elements, if you recall, had to do with "The Once"—the idea that whenever we write a narrative, we have to deal with the fact that our time is limited. Even a novel as vast as *Moby Dick* could encompass only a finite amount of time. Therefore, when you're choosing a topic, keep in mind that you cannot possibly relate the entirety of your summer vacation. At best, you can only capture a very small piece of it.

In appendix 1 of this book, you'll find an essay by one of the students I worked with that came out of her trip to Cuba. When I first started working with Megan, she had already written a couple of drafts that rather dryly compared the Cuban political system with the American political system. Her essay felt wholly impersonal, as if it had been culled from a variety of textbooks and other such sources. My first advice to her was to ditch the research paper approach altogether. (Generally, it is much easier to start from scratch than to try to fix something that is fundamentally flawed.)

As we talked, Megan began to tell me about a Cuban girl with whom she had become fast friends and about a visit they made one afternoon to a museum in Havana. As soon as I heard this, my antennae went up, for I sensed there might be a narrative lurking somewhere in that situation. And sure enough there was.

The fleeting moment in which two girls from different cultures go wandering through a museum developed into a beautiful narrative that centered on Megan, her friend, and their shared experience standing together before a painting of girls from another era who were not much older than they were. When you come to this essay in the appendix, you'll see how that brief moment is captured in this narrative with its many undercurrents and small provocative moments that allow the writer, Megan, to shine through as a person of real depth and complexity. Nothing about Megan's essay feels contrived or prepackaged. It's an original, which is just about the best thing you can say with regard to a piece of writing in this form.

Keeping in mind those two objectives of your assignment—finding a topic that will allow the real you to shine through and one that can be conveyed in a very limited amount of space—let's see how you can come up with an original, too.

Asking Questions

Writers are a curious bunch who generally like to ask questions. To fulfill this assignment as successfully as possible, you'll want to be curious, too. A good way to start things off is to ask yourself questions. Hopefully, in doing so, you'll make some discoveries that can lead you toward a suitable writing topic.

Here are some questions to start with:

- What has been the hardest thing in your life?
- What has been difficult for you to accomplish?
- At what points have you felt inadequate, and how did you deal with those feelings?

- If you had to quickly replay your life, which two or three moments would jump out ahead of all the others?
- What do you regard as your greatest victory?
- What in the world utterly fascinates you?
- Which of your relationships have you worked at the hardest?
- Have you ever made a discovery that thrilled you?
- Have you ever felt betrayed?
- What has held you back from realizing your ambitions?
- What is the funniest thing that ever happened to you?
- Have you ever felt pure rage?
- What fills you with pride?
- Have you ever felt victimized? How did you deal with it?
- What was the toughest problem that you managed to figure out?
- Have you ever faced an ethical dilemma? How did you resolve it?
- When did your mind and body feel utterly out of sync?
- When did your mind and body feel in perfect harmony?
- What is your most embarrasing moment?
- What have you done that "they" said couldn't be done?
- What object or possession holds the most meaning for you?
- If you can't sleep at night, what's keeping you up?
- Which personal weakness have you worked on the hardest?
- Which experience really pulled you out of your comfort zone?
- Who is the person that surprises you the most?
- When you close your eyes and picture a place in the world that feels special to you, which place is it?
- Have you ever experienced a genuine "life-changer"?

Now, in looking over this list, you may be shaking your head, convinced you're being led astray, right into the Valley of Clichés.

My most embarrassing moment? Are you kidding me?

Actually, I'm completely serious and also quite aware that the college essay is a form that tends to invite the cliché. That said, I would be extremely derelict in my duties if I allowed you to wander too close to the trite, the commonplace, or the stereotypical. The goal here in asking these questions is simply to find out which topics really move you. Over the course of four or five days, go over this list of questions and identify the ones you keep coming back to. If it's the Most Embarrassing, know that you're being led back to it for a reason. If there's something that's keeping you up at night, it may warrant further exploration. If the word *betrayed* is flashing on and off in your mind like a neon sign, give it room. If you find yourself pulled in any of these directions, *pay attention*.

You'll also want to see if there are connections to be made *between* your responses. For instance, I worked with a student not too long ago who answered all of the questions previously listed. She wrote that the hardest thing in her life was when her healthy, vigorous father suddenly developed a degenerative muscular disease. Then, in response to several of the other questions ("What has been difficult for me to accomplish?" "When did my mind and body feel in perfect harmony?"), she kept coming back to her experiences with dressage. For those of you who don't know, dressage is an equestrian sport that is sometimes compared to dancing or figure skating: the rider leads a horse through a series of movements such as pirouettes and trots, and is scored by a panel of judges based on style and precision.

I sensed from my interaction with this writer that she was a very controlled person, and her interest in such a controlled form as dressage confirmed that. As we went over her answers together, I asked her to consider the juxtaposition of some of those answers—the tight control demanded by dressage versus the chaos that invaded her life with the illness of her father. She wound up writing a powerful and original essay in which she did counterpoint these two themes. Could she have arrived at this insight on her own? Of course she could have, and so can you. That's why I'm suggesting that you refrain from looking at your answers in isolation from each other but, rather, that you consider the interplay of your responses.

In Step One, we identified conflict and resolution as the engine that drives all great writing, and, sure enough, that engine will be driving your writing now. Sometimes the conflict in a narrative is very obvious, as for instance when a crow has to figure out some way to get water out of a narrow-necked pitcher (*Aesop's Fables*). Sometimes the conflict is subtle, and it can take a while to figure out what's going on, as is the case with a woman whose attempt to cloak herself in illusion clashes with reality (*A Streetcar Named Desire*). Comedy too is all about conflict—from silent comedian Charlie Chaplin's fight with machinery in *Modern Times* to contemporary comedian Steve Carrell dealing with his delayed sex education in *The 40-Year-Old Virgin*. Your essay should revolve around some kind of conflict—obvious, subtle, comic, or whatever feels right to you based on why you're choosing to tell your story and which aspects of yourself you are looking to put out there.

Let me also take a moment here to address the issue of "taboo topics." Some students report to me that their college counselors tell them that they are not to write about pets (particularly the dead variety), sports injuries, or relatives. To that, I say, "Humbug." If family relationships were good enough for Sophocles, Shakespeare, and Tolstoy to write about, they should be good enough for you. Anyway, it's all about what you do with your material. You may have heard the saying, "There are no new stories, only new ways of telling them," and I think there's a lot of truth in that.

Take the example, for instance, of Asian American students. I work with a lot of them, many of whom are first-generation Americans, and they often tell variations of the same story. But that's entirely okay, because the immigrant story is one of the greatest stories ever told. Invariably, I have noticed a typical thread of tension among these children of Asian immigrants. They struggle with the dichotomy between their identities as American youths and the culture carried by their parents. They often bridle at the pressure that is brought to bear upon them—to do well and to bring honor to the family. At the same time, they work hard because they are taught by their parents to do so and because they know what's at stake. In a word, they have some real capital-C "Conflict" to write about in their admissions essays, so why shouldn't they? Does it become a cliché when these students write about this conflict? After all, how many Asian students can write about this without causing the admissions people to feel a certain sense of "been there/done that" when they see such essays over and over again?

In fact, the essays that my Asian American students create emerge as unique writings. For instance, a few years ago I was working with a student in Vancouver, BC, whose family was from Korea. He wound up couching the subject of intergenerational conflict in a very special story about getting to know an ancient, wizened fruit vendor in his neighborhood whose old-country ways were a glimpse into the traditions from which he emerged.

This student, like all the other Asian students I've worked with, managed to put a personal spin on this familiar conflict, and that's what it's all about.

I suppose the biggest hurdle for these Asian American students I work with is getting over their fear. Sometimes they are palpably afraid of failing. That's a problem when it comes to writing—at least personal writing—because there you're working without a net and you really have to let go a little. The gift for them is that in letting go, they experience something revelatory and even liberating that they can draw upon as they move ahead.

So are there any taboo topics? Well, I've been known to tell a student that it might not be the best idea to write about an eating disorder, for instance, since that problem is so epidemic on college campuses these days that it might set off warning bells for an admissions officer. That's just an example of what I personally might consider to be not a great topic choice. But it's not my role to stand between the writer and what he or she wants to write about. If the writer feels compelled to write something, it generally suggests to me that there's a good reason why, and I say go with it and let the taboo issue be damned.

In appendix 1, you'll find a number of essays that I think fulfill the college application assignment in particularly effective ways. I'd like to preview what you'll find in that section of the book by briefly discussing how the writers of these essays dealt with the issues of conflict and resolution:

- **Megan.** As mentioned previously, Megan wrote about her trip to Cuba, her friendship with a Cuban girl, and their shared experience standing before a painting of girls who were roughly their age. The conflict in her essay has to do with values and the often confusing situation of being a girl in the United States in the twenty-first century. (Think back to your list of reasons why people write, and you'll recall that one reason is to explore a value.) The resolution comes about through the insights Megan gains as a result of a cross-cultural friendship and her exposure to a work of art.

• **Jack.** Jack chose to write about a trip he made to visit his dying grandmother. (He went on to the University of Rochester, so apparently that "taboo" didn't hurt him any.) The action in Jack's story revolves around his driving two hours on his own from upstate New York to the outskirts of Boston, against the wishes of his parents, who have gone on ahead to be with his grandmother. Mostly, the narrative follows Jack as he gets very lost and asks people for directions. His grandmother only appears in the last paragraph, when Jack finally shows up at her house. The reason Jack wrote this story was to come to terms with something in his own makeup—his stubbornness—a trait that he comes to realize he has inherited from this grandmother. The conflict has to do with Jack's tendency to shoot himself in the foot; the resolution kicks in when he realizes that he comes by this trait genetically and that, in fact, his stubbornness carries a positive charge as well as a negative one.

• **Hannah.** Hannah's family suffered a major trauma in the year before she applied to college. Her older sister was suddenly stricken with a brain tumor. Although the tumor turned out to be benign, its sudden appearance was a terrifying event that caused everyone in the family to reexamine their lives. Hannah tells this story through the lens of a summer camp experience, as she rehearses a scene in a camp production of the Thornton Wilder play *Our Town*. She is playing Emily, Wilder's protagonist, who wrestles with the meaning of life and death. Hannah's conflict is an elemental one—Can she handle the terrible knowledge that human beings are mortal?—and her resolution comes about through the cathartic experience of playing a character who is dealing with the very same issue.

- **Eve.** Eve had a substantial conflict going on in her life— she had pretty much botched her high school career. She followed high school immediately with a trip to Italy, and, when she returned and decided to apply to college, she figured she'd write about that trip for her essay. As she progressed from draft to draft, she had to change the essay's orientation from a travelogue of her trip to a travelogue of her soul.

- **Matt.** Matt, the author of a "dead pet" story (another supposed taboo, but this writer went on to Oberlin), had experienced a difficult senior year. A clash with a crazy coach left him feeling very burned out on his high school soccer team. As if that weren't enough, he accidentally ran over his beloved dog on the Fourth of July—two days before he was set to go to soccer camp. Either of these subjects could be worked up into an essay, but the fact that these two themes came together in one unfortunate but highly dramatic event made it inevitable that he would choose to somehow turn this tale into a college essay. The question was how to unify it, and how to avoid the maudlin. It was quite a complicated task to sort out the conflict and resolution in this essay, but, when you come to it in the appendix, I think you might agree with me that he succeeded.

- **Victor.** Victor was a brilliant math and science student who didn't particularly like to write—particularly not about himself. We went back and forth on the discovery process, poring over his answers to the exploratory questions, and when he happened to mention something about eating ice cream with his grandfather in the back of a dusty barbershop in Taiwan, the little hairs on the back of my neck began to tingle. He found a very special way to write about a person who had an important influence on his life.

All of these writers did what you, as a writer, have to do: Ask *why?* Why do I want to write about this topic? Why does it touch me? Often, when students come to me, they have a topic in mind, but they don't understand what has motivated them to choose it. Hannah knew why she wanted to write about her sister's illness— because it was such a huge event in her life and her feelings about it were still so raw. But Jack wasn't clear why he chose to write about the trip to visit his grandmother in Boston. He thought that maybe he was going to be telling a story about a series of wrong turns, blind alleys, and miscellaneous misadventures—a comedy, perhaps?—but it was only after he did some digging that he got to the *why* of the piece. It was then that he realized that the trip and the manner in which he undertook it were expressive of who he is and were therefore worthy of serious examination.

Ultimately, the one who will answer the *why* question will be you. After all, it's your story. That's why you should never rely on your parents or your brother or your sister to come up with the topic for *your* college essay. They're likely to say something like, "Why don't you write about that time you found $100 in a wallet in the supermarket and you turned it over to the manager?" They might think that (a) it's a good story and (b) it casts you in a positive light, and they may be right, but that doesn't mean that this story is going to express the kind of conflict and resolution that you—and we—are looking for. It's not necessarily going to be the kind of story where you can step back and ask *why* and come up with a good answer. "Because my mother told me to" is not a good answer.

You have to spend the time—asking yourself the questions I've listed on pages 33 and 34—to find the story within you that's aching to come out. It's a story that could be sad, funny, angry, confused, doubting, yearning, regretful, or a combination of any and all of these emotions. But whatever it is, it must capture the essence of who you are, how you see the world, and how you fit into the world. The good news is that everyone has such a story. "I can't think of one" is just a stage, and you will get beyond it.

Recap

1. The main reasons why college application essays fail are that they're predictable, overly sentimental, poorly told, or too self-promoting.

2. Give yourself the time you need to write a good essay. This task should not be rushed.

3. Start brainstorming by considering the reasons why people write in the first place. To amuse, to confess, to connect—these are just some of many reasons.

4. Plan on presenting yourself in a good light—not as a flawless person, but as a real one.

5. When choosing your topic, keep in mind the time limitations of a narrative. That is to say, don't plan on re-creating your *entire* summer vacation.

6. Ask yourself probing questions to act as "prompts" for your essay writing.

7. Understand that your essay should revolve around some point of conflict and should offer some kind of resolution.

8. Everyone has a story to tell. It's just a matter of discovering what that story is.

STEP THREE

Point of View

Once you settle on a topic, you'll immediately be faced with other important decisions. One of your first considerations concerns point of view. As a high school student of some seniority, you should be familiar with this literary term. Briefly defined, *point of view* is the vantage point from which the writer passes the narrative to the reader. There are three factors that determine point of view: person, tense, and number.

Person

With regard to the *person* aspect of point of view, writers have three options to choose from: first person, second person, and third person.

FIRST PERSON

When using a first-person point of view, the narrator becomes a character in the story—often the main one. Think of Holden Caulfield in *The Catcher in the Rye* and you'll recall how memorably that first-person voice jumps out at you from the opening lines:

> If you really want to hear about it, the first thing you'll prob-
> ably want to know is where I was born, and what my lousy
> childhood was like, and how my parents were occupied and
> all before they had me, and all that David Copperfield kind
> of crap, but I don't feel like going into it, if you want to know
> the truth.

That kind of voice has been used—usually not as originally or as effectively—in countless young adult novels since. A first-person narrator can also act as a lesser player in the piece—more of an observer who relates the story of the main players. Think of Nick Carraway in *The Great Gatsby* or Marlow in *Lord Jim*—observers and chroniclers who tell the story from a distance. In writing your college application essay, you will most likely use a first-person point of view. Very few of the students I've worked with have used anything else.

SECOND PERSON

A second-person point of view is not one that you will normally (or perhaps ever) encounter. It will strike you as exceedingly odd sounding, and, as a technique, it is usually used experimentally. The second-person narration feels very detached, with descrip-tions that sound almost clinical. Imagine, for instance, writing a college essay *about* writing a college essay, told from a second-person point of view.

> You sit down at the desk. You look at your paper. You
> freeze. What can you possibly tell these people that they
> haven't heard before? You go to the refrigerator. You eat
> a yogurt. You eat another yogurt. You return to your desk.

It's interesting, yes, and may well capture that awful sense of desperation that can surround this task, but it's extremely difficult to sustain, even in a piece of only six hundred fifty words.

THIRD PERSON

A third-person point of view is the one that readers most frequently encounter. Think of the Bible, and you'll immediately hear that voice, as in the creation of Eve, depicted in Genesis 2:22:

> And the Lord God formed the rib which he had taken from the man into a woman, and brought her unto the man.

Now, think of a book that many of you have probably had to read: Nathaniel Hawthorne's *The Scarlet Letter*. Remember this?

> Hester Prynne's term of confinement was now at an end. Her prison-door was thrown open, and she came forth into the sunshine, which, falling on all alike, seemed, to her sick and morbid heart, as if meant for no other purpose than to reveal the scarlet letter on her breast.

Both the Bible and *The Scarlet Letter* are written in the third person. Third-person narration can be *omniscient*—meaning that the narrator knows everything about everyone and can pop in and out of a character's head at will—or it can be limited, as in a third-person narration that closely follows the thoughts of only one character. It is unlikely that you would choose to tell your personal narrative from a third-person point of view. To do so would create a feeling of distance that would be confusing in your personal narrative. For instance, imagine your account of your river raft trip in the third person:

Three guys, heading down the river, holding on for dear life as they hit the rapids, the white foam in their faces. . . .

You'd go through your narrative and then, at the end, you'd probably want to pull back and say something like this:

And one of those three guys was me.

Now it's not impossible to imagine a personal narrative that would work in the third person, but, for our purposes, we can assume that you won't be headed in that direction. If you do choose that direction, however, you'll have all the same narrative problems to address: "The Once," The Extraordinary vs. The Ordinary, Tension and Conflict, and The Point.

For our purposes, then, as I've said, let's assume that you're going to use a first-person point of view to tell your personal narrative. Your opening sentence will then sound something like this:

- I couldn't believe it when I saw him coming through the door.
- I've always been known for my stubbornness.
- My dog just lay there, like a broken toy.

These are not great sentences—in fact, I would urge you *not* to open your essay by comparing your dead dog to a broken toy— but, even so, you can see how powerful the "I" voice is. It feels intimate and confessional, and we tend to pay attention to it.

Tense

Tense refers to the time frame in which the narrative unfolds. Your choices on this front will always be the same: past, present, or future.

Many students choose to take a reflective stance in their personal narratives. They look back to how they used to be—relating an incident or anecdote from their past—and reflect on it in the present to show how they've learned and matured. Accordingly, the tense in such narratives shifts around. The first paragraph might find the narrator in the present—"I'm a different person now than I was a year ago"—while the middle paragraphs will hearken back to the past, with the last paragraph returning the narrator to the present again. Alternatively, the narrative might be set entirely in the past, until the last paragraph, when the narrator shifts to the present for the reflective wrap-up. All writers need to be careful, however, that they don't jump around with their tenses *within* a particular time frame. In other words, when you're writing about the past, you must maintain a past tense, and when you're writing about the future, you must maintain a future tense.

Your narrative could also be set entirely in the past, and, if it's powerful enough, the reader will not miss the reflective note. It's useful to realize that the past can be written with a very "present" feeling. Let's look at an essay that is set entirely in the past:

The first thing I noticed was that all the trees were bare. As I drove up the hill to Camp Shiloh, I remembered how the maple trees, arching toward each other from either side of the road, formed a natural canopy that always felt cool. Now, in October, all the leaves were gone and what once felt cool suddenly felt cold.

I parked at the office and trudged up toward Bunk 3, where I had been in charge of twelve ten-year-olds last summer. It was a good summer, full of laughter and hard work, but that seemed like ages ago now.

I stepped into the bunk. It was very dim, almost spooky. In the shadows I could make out stripped metal cots and a broom standing in the corner.

"Hello?" I called.

"Over here," a voice returned.

Stepping forward, I could make out Amy, my co-counselor from last summer, sitting on one of the beds. We had made plans to meet here and then go on to the meeting together.

"Hey," I said.

She looked at me. We weren't the best of friends, but we had a lot in common.

"You okay?" I asked.

She shook her head, and then burst into tears. She and Evan were very close.

"I'm sorry," she said, shaking her head.

"No. That's okay," I answered, not knowing what else to say.

Together, in silence, we walked up to the nurse's office, where the meeting was being held. A bunch of the other counselors were already there—Ronnie, Pat, D.J., Carmen. Everyone but Evan. We sat on the floor in a circle, not quite looking into each other's eyes, knowing that we were here for some group "therapy" but having no expectations that anything was going to make us feel better.

"Does anyone want to start?" asked Michelle, the camp nurse.

Nobody said anything until Amy finally spoke up. Of all of us, she was probably the closest to Evan, but he was my special friend, too.

"Why did he do it?" Amy asked. "Why?"

"Maybe he thought he didn't have a choice," said Carmen.

"You're telling me he had no choice?" Amy nearly shouted, and then she turned away and buried her face in her crossed arms.

Evan was unique. He was the funniest person I ever met. He always saw the absurd side to any situation, and he had crazy spiky red hair and a million freckles. He looked like the kid on a cereal box—not like someone who would kill himself. And not knowing why he would do such a thing was the hardest part of all.

"Jen? Is there anything you want to say?"

Somehow I'd lost all sense of time and didn't even know how long we'd been sitting there. All I knew was that my friend was gone and so was some part of me.

"No," I murmured. "Nothing."

I looked through the window at the bare trees and wondered if I'd ever get that part of me back.

While this narrative takes place in the past, it somehow has a "present" feeling. How is that accomplished? Well, for one thing, it features dialogue throughout, and dialogue can be an extremely potent tool. People like to hear people talk—it makes them sit up and take notice and conveys a feeling of freshness and immediacy. Later on in this book, I will provide some specific pointers that will help you create effective dialogue, because ineffective dialogue is every bit as deadly as good dialogue is invigorating.

The preceding essay uses a few other tricks to break up the past tense. While the tense in this sample narrative almost appears to shift at various moments, it actually remains securely moored in the past. This essay has no tense inconsistencies—a problem you must always be on the outlook for in your writing—but it does play with tense. Consider the sentence at the end of the second paragraph: "It was a good summer, full of laughter and hard work, but that seemed like ages ago now." While there is no tense inconsistency, the word *now* creates the *illusion* of a present-tense feeling, and this helps to energize a past-tense piece.

The writer of this narrative might have chosen to end it with a shift to the present tense. Something like this:

> I looked through the window at the bare trees and wondered if I'd ever get that part of me back. Now, a year later, I know that I have gotten it back. The loss wounded me, but my spirit is recovering. Evan would have wanted that.

That approach could have worked, but I think the point is made well enough without having to go into that present-tense, reflective mode. How will you make choices like that? By reading your various versions out loud and listening to them carefully, and then giving them to other people to read and paying attention to their input. That's the way a piece of writing "cooks"—there are no shortcuts. (Which is exactly why you need to give an assignment like this the amount of "cooking time" it deserves.)

Are there any other little tricks going on in this piece? As a matter of fact, yes. Consider the opening. It starts out in medias res, plunging you right into the middle of the action. This "plunging" creates a real feeling of immediacy and grabs the reader's attention.

Interestingly, in working with student writers on their college application essays, I have found that I can often counsel them to get rid of their opening sentences with nothing lost and no harm done. Those first sentences are usually dull and expository. For the sample essay you just read, they would probably sound something like this:

> Last summer, I was a counselor at Camp Shiloh. It was a very good summer, but everything that was good about it faded in the face of a terrible tragedy.

Is there anything wrong with either of those sentences above? No, as sentences go, they're fine. On the other hand, they're not going to make a reader snap to attention—particularly not one who has been plowing through hundreds of other essays. And the decision to plunge right into the action can also save you a lot of words. When it comes to the college admissions essay, that famous dictum of design, "Less is more," rules the day. As you must realize, you are severely limited by your space allotment here. Six hundred fifty words is really just the blink of an eye. So everything you put down should be there for the express purpose of making an impact on your reader.

Now let me anticipate two questions you may want to ask: Does this sample essay present the writer in a good light? Does it make her seem too depressed? Some people might shy away from dealing with such difficult material. My feeling is that through the very act of writing, the writer has shown that she is processing the loss she has experienced. I think it's a brave story that still has a ways to go, but I think ultimately it will become a piece that will make an impact on the admissions counselor who reads it.

OTHER TENSE CHOICES

Getting back to the tense issue, as I said, there are three choices. You can use past tense, as I've just shown, and that will most likely be your choice. The other choices available to a writer are present tense, future tense, or some combination thereof. It's quite unlikely that you would use future tense—I *will* go there; I *will* do that—unless you want to give your essay a certain sci-fi flair, but writing your entire piece in the present tense is conceivable. Listen to what the story of Jen at Camp Shiloh would sound like in the present tense—at least a piece of it:

> The first thing I notice is that all the trees are bare. As I drive up the hill to Camp Shiloh, I remember how the maple trees, arching toward each other from either side

of the road, formed a natural canopy that always felt cool. Now, in October, all the leaves are gone and what once felt cool suddenly feels cold.

I park at the office and trudge up toward Bunk 3, where I had been in charge of twelve ten-year-olds last summer. It was a good summer, full of laughter and hard work, but that seems like ages ago now.

I step into the bunk. It's very dim, almost spooky. In the shadows I can make out stripped metal cots and a broom standing in the corner.

"Hello?" I call.

"Over here," a voice returns.

So what do you think? Have we gained anything from using a present-tense point of view? Does it feel more immediate, more interesting, more attention-grabbing? Maybe so. The present tense *is* kind of interesting here, but would I choose to go with it? I really wouldn't know until I finished a draft and compared it with the past-tense version—assuming I was ambitious enough to try it both ways. In a somber, reflective piece like the Camp Shiloh essay, I would probably go with the past tense just because it would be more consistent with the mood. If I were writing about a river trip in Colorado that I took last summer, I might use the present tense, just to better convey the sense of excitement, and then at the end, I might switch into the past tense with a bit of reflection—something like, "That was the best trip I ever took. It really changed the way I think about myself and nature." One of the really fun things about writing is making these kinds of choices. And, again, you need to sit with your piece, read it out loud, give it to others to read, and take your time with it in order to make sure your choices are the right ones.

Number

The other aspect of point of view that requires some kind of decision is *number*. The number will be either singular or plural.

You will be using first-person singular if the narrator is you and you are referring to yourself:

I park at the office and trudge up toward Bunk 3, where I had been in charge of twelve ten-year-olds last summer.

If somehow you were telling your narrative from a group perspective, you would use first-person plural. For instance, if you wanted to convey the sense of a group of people going on a raft ride, your narrative might read like this:

We held on to the sides of the raft, waiting for the next thrill.

In the narrative that you are writing for your college application, it is most likely that, even if you use the first-person plural for part of it, you will introduce a first-person singular voice at some later point in the essay, as in:

We held on to the sides of the raft, waiting for the next thrill. I had never felt so scared—or so exhilarated—in my entire life.

Clearly, it's a simple thing to move from the first-person plural to the first-person singular, so think of that as an option that's fully available to you.

As for the third-person singular, it would sound something like this:

She parked at the office and trudged up toward Bunk 3, where she had been in charge of twelve ten-year-olds last summer.

It is highly unlikely that you would use this voice, or the third-person plural, which would sound like this:

They held on to the sides of the raft, waiting for the next thrill.

If you chose to be experimental, you might give these third-person number options a try, but, chances are, you wouldn't stick with it. It would only distance you from your reader, which is exactly what you're trying to avoid in this context. You want your essay to make as strong and direct a connection as possible, between you and the admissions officer reading it and that third-person voice is not going to bring the two of you close.

Hopefully, Steps two and three have given you a handle on two of your biggest issues—your topic and your point of view. Let's now move ahead and get to work on your first draft.

Recap

1. Point of view is the vantage point from which the writer passes the narrative to the reader.

2. There are three factors that determine point of view: tense, person, and number.

3. Your choice of tense is past, present, or future. You will most likely use past, but you could use present.

4. With regard to person, there are three options to choose from: first person, second person, and third person.

5. In your college application essay, you will most likely use a first-person narration.

6. Third-person narration can be omniscient or limited and may be useful at certain times.

7. In terms of number, you will most likely use the first-person singular.

8. Consider starting your narrative in the middle of the action. It can create a feeling of immediacy and can save precious words.

Getting It Down

There are many ways to approach your writing task; as writer, your job is to find the one that suits you best. Some writers find that their output is more productive if they meet a daily quota. Come what may, they'll write three hundred or five hundred or one thousand words in a sitting, and then, if they're very successful, they'll spend the rest of the day in meetings with their agents, their editors, or their personal trainers. Other writers have a more driven nature. Fueled by Romantic notions of the artist as a tortured soul, they have feverishly creative sessions that can last into the wee hours of the morning.

Regardless of the time of day you like to write, it's important to note that writing does require a certain kind of environment in which you can *hear yourself.* One way to begin is by clearing your head. Unfortunately, most of the student writers that I work with have seriously overloaded heads. For the most part, they are high school seniors who are up to their necks in responsibilities. They have schoolwork to keep up, extracurricular activities to attend to, standardized tests to prepare for, colleges to visit, and, of course, applications to complete. By the time they get around to the admissions essay, their heads are ready to pop.

So the first thing they—and you—have to do is take a deep breath and find a quiet place. That's how the essay-writing process begins. (Let me say, the place should be *relatively* quiet, because a lot of people like to write in a Starbucks or whatever and that's fine, but there's a difference between a Starbucks, by yourself, and trying to write in the family room while your brother is playing *Grand Theft Auto*.)

Here's my advice: go to that quiet place. Let it be a secluded section of a park or library or rooftop or any place where you can hear yourself think. Turn off all electronics—*including your cell phone*. Many people today are deeply afraid of spending even a moment in such quietude. They are apparently afraid of their own inner self. But you mustn't be if you're going to commit to the act of writing. The best writing—particularly writing of a deeply personal nature, which is what you are being asked to do with the assignment ahead of you—springs from that inner self.

I once read an interview with writer Joseph Heller, author of the classic novel *Catch-22*, in which he described his writing process. He said he got his best ideas when he would lie down for a "nap." It wasn't a real nap, in which the goal is to actually fall asleep, but, rather, he was describing a "nap-like" experience in which he put himself into a kind of half-sleep. In that half-sleep, the subconscious part of his mind went to work and sometimes (not always) presented images, thoughts, and situations that he could think about when he returned to a fully awake state.

We get so hung up in daily life with issues like getting to practice on time or meeting a deadline on a term paper or remembering to call Grandma on her birthday that we don't make room for the deeper thoughts that are required for this important writing assignment. So when you're getting ready to start this assignment, go take a "nap" (sort of). Let yourself think about the things in your life that have been hardest for you or that moment in your life when you felt pure rage or when your body and mind felt in perfect sync. Lie there, in that half-sleep, and see what kinds of thoughts, images, situations, and words bubble up.

Remember too that while retreating to a quiet place may be a good thing to do, you might still encounter problems along the way. I'm talking here about resistance, a big part of writing and one that can be potentially disabling. Let's have a look at the issue of resistance more closely.

Whoever Said It Was Easy?

Writing is, by its very nature, a difficult experience, one that is laden with challenge for almost all writers, the professionals as well as the novices. One of the main reasons why resistance kicks in is because every writer—novice and pro alike—knows in a deep and painful way that one's writing effort will somehow fall short of the mark. When it comes to writing, there is no such thing as perfection. There can be a perfect square, a perfect omelet, a perfectly pitched baseball game, but perfect writing? Don't believe it. Writing is all about the tension between vision and execution. Think about it. Haven't you sat down to write a paper, having set up the whole thing in your mind, and when it came time to actually put down the words, something happened . . . or didn't. Those words just wouldn't come . . . or else they did, but in an inarticulate jumble. Your thoughts seemed shallow. Your prose felt doughy. Sentences that should have been easy to write suddenly became Gordian knots, impossible to untangle. Well, guess what?

That kind of thing happens to all writers.

Even though I've been a professional writer for more than thirty years, I can still get stuck on a sentence, and sometimes I have to ask my wife, also a writer, to bail me out. Fortunately, at this point in my life, such failings don't throw me. Just as your foot can fall asleep and won't listen to what your brain is telling it to do, so too can your mind go blank or foggy, and suddenly it won't know how to string words together.

Fortunately, there are excellent solutions for these writing problems, and they're called *drafts*. In the course of writing your college application essay, you will go through a series of drafts—let's say three drafts and a polish—and sidestepping these stages of the process is *not* an option. No one gets this assignment right the first time out of the gate. It simply doesn't happen that way. So, with that understood, let's look at some practical ways to get started.

Freewriting

Gathering raw material is a challenge that all writers face. Where are the ideas going to come from? Experienced writers trust that the raw materials will somehow make their way to the page, given time, patience, and fortitude. Novice writers may not trust that such a miracle will ever take place, and so resistance, spurred on by fear, may kick in. Most likely, this resistance will assume the form of procrastination—putting off until tomorrow what you can do today.

Procrastination is a truly insidious self-sabotaging behavior because it's so easy to convince yourself you *will* get on task, but then, before you know it, time goes by and you've painted yourself into a corner. Your essay is due in forty-eight hours and that simply doesn't leave you sufficient time to get the job done well. The situation calls for a drastic remedy, and one such remedy you may want to try is called *freewriting*.

With freewriting, your only rule is that you set aside a prescribed amount of time—ten minutes feels about right for most people—and you *just write*. You don't concern yourself with spelling, punctuation, syntax, tense, word choice, or any of those other things that can go wrong with a piece of writing. There is no censorship and no self-criticism. The writing merely happens—in a rush, without stopping—for the set amount of time.

Whenever I ask a class or some other group of students to engage in freewriting, shock and confusion usually ensues. It's as if the principal has said it's okay to have food fights in the cafeteria. There's often an outburst of giggling or perhaps a rash of tense questions from those students who need clearly structured assignments. Once this confusion has passed and the students get down to work, there will be a fair share of those in the room whose expressions suggest that they're involved in a kind of heavy lifting. You can almost hear the grunts and groans, but what these students may not realize on any conscious level is that the arduousness of their task is all about the *shedding* of the burden. Casting off a lifetime's supply of rules can feel like work too, particularly in those first moments when you fear that you're being plunged into chaos.

As I watch the students settle into their assignment, I'll see that some of them remain fixed in a mode of resistance—or else they're experimenting with resistance, which is a highly recommended course of action. For instance, they might spend the entire time writing one phrase over and over again—*This is stupid This is stupid This is stupid*—not realizing until it's pointed out to them that the act of writing such a phrase over and over might constitute an act of liberation in and of itself. Those who genuinely get into the spirit of the freewriting—and most people do after their first encounter—will very likely feel exhilarated as they enter this brave new world free of constraints.

When the ten minutes are up and the exercise is over, I will point out that the freewriting has functioned as a kind of limbering exercise. Down the line, rules will return, for some measure of rules is inevitable when it comes to writing, but, for now, the freewriting can stretch you, loosen you up, and get you ready for the real work ahead. In some instances, viable seeds for further writing exploration may also be culled from the chaff of your freewriting. Perhaps a certain phrase captures your attention. Maybe a metaphor grabs your interest. Even one good word can do a lot to send you in a fruitful direction. But even if nothing concrete comes of it, the calisthenic nature of the freewriting still renders it worthwhile.

Freewriting is something you can do entirely on your own. It requires no special equipment, no operating license, no proctor, no judge, and no jury. You do it and it's done with. Later on, if you get stuck during your first-draft stage, you can always freewrite some more. It's perfectly fine to do it as much as you want, and it beats the heck out of procrastination, which comes with a hefty price tag and leaves you feeling rotten in the morning.

PS An Idea

While the principle of *less is more* is a good one to guide you toward your ultimate product, at this first-draft stage you're still trying to amass your raw materials. Being stingy with your ideas at this point will leave you without enough to work with.

As a young writer, Noah, my older son, suffered from such stinginess. He had a nice feeling for language, but his writing assignments tended to be as highly compacted as owl pellets. If his teacher asked for five hundred words, my son would always weigh in with a first draft of three hundred or, on a good day, three hundred fifty. From then on, he was in full padding mode—one word at a time. Eventually, he lost this parsimony and became a more fluid writer. I think, in his case, what most helped him overcome his problem was getting into the habit of writing emails. As he relaxed with writing in this loose, nonthreatening format, he was able to produce more.

My son's experience suggests what could be a useful exercise for those of you who are feeling gummed up and resistant to writing. Try doing a draft of your essay as if you were writing a letter to a friend—or an email to a friend, if letter writing feels too alien. The conversational nature of this kind of writing can help you loosen up, relax, and actually produce a good amount of prose that can then be trimmed, massaged, and otherwise reworked to meet the more formal standards of the college application essay. Writing a draft by pretending it's a series of text messages probably won't yield much material you can use in your final essay, but hey—if you think that will do the trick and loosen you up, far be it from me to stand in your way.

Those Six Hundred Fifty Words

In most instances, the college application essay will be a piece of writing around six hundred fifty words long. Now this is not, by any standards, a lot of words. Overwhelming length is hardly the issue that is leading you to procrastinate here. What, then, is the issue? In fact, there may be any number of issues, including the following:

1. **Fear of failure.** When you sit down to write, you're afraid. That's okay—as I've said, most writers feel that way. Vision and execution are typically poles apart, and that's why we go through a series of drafts—to bring those poles closer together. The closer we can bring them, the better we feel about our writing and ourselves. Understanding that this is the purpose of writing drafts—to make vision and execution come closer together—will help you control the fear of failure that can lead to so much resistance.

2. **A lot is at stake.** Here we're talking about a fear of failure that's even more global in nature. It's not just about the writing falling short—it's about *you* falling short. What if you're not good enough to get into the college of your choice? What if you don't get into your second, third, or fourth choice? What if you aren't admitted into *any* college? That happens, doesn't it? Well, yes, on occasion such dire disappointments do take place, but filling your head with doomsday scenarios is only the mind's nasty little way of keeping you from the task at hand. After all, it's easier to fixate on all the bad things that *might* happen than it is to focus on the one thing that absolutely *needs* to happen.

3. **It's tough stuff.** Your third route into procrastination may come as a result of the subject matter you've chosen to write about. Consider the setup: I'm encouraging you to select a writing topic that has a considerable degree of conflict connected to it. If you were merely planning to tout your achievements, telling your reader how you've been captain of the tennis team/editor in chief of the student newspaper/ first violinist in the orchestra, then perhaps you wouldn't experience much in the way of resistance at all. You'd bask in the rosy glow of your own dazzling reflection, and everything would be right with the world. Although it might be nice

to operate without resistance, I suspect it would result in a product that would ultimately be boring for your reader. And that's not a choice you can afford to make—easy for you, boring for your audience—so you'd better stick with conflict. Therefore, instead of writing about the three hundred consecutive winning matches you've enjoyed as captain of the tennis team, try writing about the championship match that somehow slipped away, and how you came to terms with this rare instance of defeat. That's a story that might hold your reader's interest and allow that reader to see you as a living, breathing, three-dimensional human being. But, even if you fully understand that the nature of this writing assignment necessitates that you grapple with some real conflict, that doesn't mean you're going to *enjoy* it. Difficult feelings are, by logical extension, difficult to write about. It's hard work to bring insight to your disappointments, frustrations, shortcomings, or painful life lessons. But that's the business at hand, if, in fact, you agree that conflict is a critical aspect of this assignment.

So now that we've reviewed three of the main reasons why this writing task is so often fraught with resistance, let's step back and look at those six hundred fifty words. This amount is, by all accounts, a manageable goal, and manageable goals are best achieved when we exercise a certain amount of will. Always remember that self-discipline is a force that can be every bit as powerful as resistance.

Seasoned writers use little tricks to counter resistance and foster discipline. Some rely on certain habits and routines to set them up for the difficult work that lies ahead. They may need three cups of coffee, a walk with the dog, or a look at the paper. Such habits and routines can relax writers and ease them into the more significant routine of the writing itself.

As I said at the beginning of this chapter, many writers link their writing routine to some kind of quota. Whether the quota is three hundred or five hundred or one thousand words a day is up to the writer. The point is that if this quota is met with some kind of real discipline—let's say four or five or six days a week—then the words will really start to add up and, over the course of time, those three hundred words a day could even turn into a book. (The average manuscript for a novel is something like seventy thousand words, so do the math. Three hundred words a day in two hundred thirty three days could become a seventy-thousand-word novel in less than a year.)

Now think about this: your college application essay is *not* a novel. It's not even a short story. It's a mere six hundred fifty words. So why not follow the example of those writers who have been at it for a while and set a quota for yourself? Tell yourself that you will *not* go to bed until you have written . . . what? Twenty-five words? Fifty words? One hundred words? It's up to you. You're in charge, after all. But no matter what quota you set for yourself, the very act of setting the goal should, by all rights, work toward breaking down procrastination. Another helpful note: Lower the bar when you're setting your quota. It's better to have a quota you can safely meet, even if it's a small one, than a larger quota you fail to meet. Such failures will only deplete your confidence, which can lead to even more procrastination. And who needs that?

The Morning After

At some point, all your quotas will add up, you will find yourself with a finished first draft, and then comes the time to examine what you've written. This experience can be deeply sobering. Here are four confidence-building methods to turn to on the morning after, when the first draft of your college application essay isn't looking too good:

1. **Congratulate yourself.** What you did last night was no small thing. You confronted resistance and, using discipline like a chair and a whip, you backed that resistance into a corner. This is something to feel good about, and feeling good about something will go a long way toward enabling you to finish the job. Be aware, however, that the beast is lying in wait for you. Resistance will continue to crop up all along the way, from one draft to the next.

2. **Suspend judgment.** All living creatures respond favorably to a nurturing environment. Plants grow best with proper measures of light, moisture, and pH level. Writers too develop best when they are protected, to some degree at least, from harsh environmental factors. Telling yourself that you are the stupidest and worst writer who ever lived is a harsh environmental factor. Forget the abuse and instead find something in your writing that deserves commendation. My guess is it's there. It might be an image. It might be a metaphor. It might be an honest emotion. Look for it, find it, and carry it over to your next draft. Ultimately, even this good "something" might not make the final cut, but, for now at least, identifying that good "something" will help bolster your spirits.

3. **Get other readings.** Claiming ownership over your writing is important, but so is hearing opinions from other people. It's never too soon to round up your readers, but you have to be careful to assess their relative merits. If your mother has always showered you with equally enthusiastic praise for every sun catcher you ever made at summer camp and every trumpet solo you ever butchered your way through, then she might be a great mom for all the unconditional love she has to offer, but not the best source for useful critical input.

Look around and you're bound to find someone else who can serve in this capacity. An aunt, an uncle, a neighbor, a friend, a teacher (and not necessarily your English teacher)—someone who can say, "I like this, but I don't understand that" is what you're looking for. By the end of this book, *you* should become that kind of useful reader for yourself, but along the way, input from intelligent, kind, and thoughtful sources can be extremely valuable.

4. **Hold nothing sacred.** Macabre as it may seem, I have to keep going back to that "kill your babies" advice. I want you to understand that writing is really about process. If you feel after your first draft that your essay is going absolutely nowhere, then you might choose to jettison it—cut your losses, as it were—and move on to a new essay. That's a perfectly okay thing to do, as long as it's a decision you reach out of some kind of critical judgment rather than sheer panic. Even if you stay with the piece through a second, third, and even fourth draft, you might find that by the time you've reached the end, almost nothing has survived from the beginning. Not only is that a perfectly normal course of events, but it can also indicate that you've actually done an enormous amount of good work—killing your babies as the need presented itself. In counseling you to hold nothing sacred, I'm directing you squarely to the idea of process. Once you understand that writing *is* process, you will take comfort in knowing that essays do not occur miraculously or through some kind of divine intervention, but are the products that you reach at the end of the process. Down the road, if writing genuinely comes to interest you, you will find that the pleasure of the process more than makes up for the fear and resistance.

A lot to think about in this chapter? Indeed. But now it's time to get back to work and put more of your essay down on paper.

Recap

1. Writing always falls short of perfection. It's about the tension between vision and execution.

2. To initiate the writing process, find a quiet place where you can hear yourself think.

3. Drafts are a necessary part of the process. Plan on at least three drafts and a polish for your college application essay.

4. Freewriting—writing without any rules for a prescribed period of time—is a good "limbering" exercise that can get your creative juices flowing.

5. If you're stuck, try writing your essay as a letter or an email to a friend.

6. Procrastination can occur because of fear of failure, the realization that a lot is at stake, and the resistance that comes with writing about deeply personal issues.

7. Try setting a quota of a certain amount of words per day to stimulate your writing output.

8. Know that your first draft will probably fall short of your expectations. Congratulate yourself for the work you've done, suspend judgment, get other readings if you wish, and hold nothing sacred.

"Big Picture" Editing

As discussed in the previous step, vision and execution often fall poles apart—particularly at the start of the writing process. The purpose of writing drafts is to bring vision and execution closer together, but sometimes they stubbornly refuse to come into alignment. In this first-draft stage, you're looking at the "big picture," trying to figure out what went wrong and why your vision and execution have not lined up as they should have. What you'll discover is that there are many ways for your desired product to fall short, but this is not an invitation to despair. Generally speaking, these problems—once you're able to identify them—can be corrected.

Common Errors

Once they've completed their first drafts, most of my student writers find they have fallen into one or more common traps. Allow me to introduce you to some of the typical pitfalls.

CONCEPT

Perhaps you'll find that your biggest problem is the underlying concept of your piece. You thought it would be hilarious to write a scathing satire of the college application essay from the point of view of a chimpanzee, but somehow, when you read it over in the morning, the joke fell flat. No harm done. Chalk it up to the old "college try," and move on to an altogether new six hundred fifty words. But wait! you cry. You've already spent three nights working on this piece. Sorry, friend, but I can't be that sympathetic. I've written novels that haven't worked out. The only thing you can do with a big "big picture" problem is cut your losses and forge ahead.

PRESENTATION

Sometimes the concept is fine, but the treatment falls flat. Maybe your language was tight and stilted. Perhaps you relied on clichés to carry your piece along, or maybe you went overboard with description, oozing metaphors from every pore. Problems of this nature are often remediable, and you may be able to tackle them after letting your piece sit for a while and then going back to it or by getting readings from other people whose critical judgment you trust.

STRUCTURE

Is the problem structural in nature? Did you spend too much time setting up the situation and then had to play catch-up to bring the piece to a close? Your reader—in this case, you—comes away feeling unsatisfied, as if there hasn't been enough to eat on the plate. You might try outlining your finished piece; when you see it in its skeleton form, the structural flaws may pop out for you.

TONE

There are other ways your execution can undermine your vision. Perhaps your tone is all wrong. This happens a lot with the college application essay. In an attempt to bring "importance" to the undertaking, some writers overindulge in ten-letter words, choosing "magnanimous" for "generous" or "euphonious" for "tuneful." Quite transparently, writer and thesaurus have been joined at the hip. While a few well-chosen "Sunday words" can enhance your writing, the fact is that a mass of polysyllabic words will soon present itself as an impenetrable thicket.

Another way you can err on tone is by being flip or sarcastic where openness and honesty are called for. I often see essays in which the language smacks of the kind of brash, jokey lingo found in generic young adult novels. The writers of such essays start out with constructions like, "If you want to know how a person can screw himself up, ask yours truly" or "Little did I know that my birthday was going to turn out to be a nightmare in living color." These kinds of constructions, trying so hard to be bright, quickly tarnish, leaving the reader wishing that a real human being would come along with something sincere to say.

In terms of tonal errors, another common mishap is the maudlin sob fest—an essay that's foolishly and tearfully sentimental. For some reason, maudlin essays often have to do with those dead pets we've already alluded to. "Gazing down upon Elmo's limp, lifeless carcass, I felt the life drain out of me and knew in the deepest recesses of my soul that life as I had known it would never be the same again." You can almost hear the organ chords swelling in the background.

Another word I'll use to describe a product I haven't liked is *smarmy*—it describes something that's hypocritically, complacently, or effusively earnest. I tend to encounter smarmy essays from those students who have approached the first draft as an invitation to promote their accomplishments. The dramatic action is sacrificed to make room for sentences like this: "As president of the Student Union, an office that I have held for three straight years, possibly accomplishing more of my agenda than any other student that has held this post in the history of our school, I was shocked to discover that the administration was not going to replace the broken soda machine in the cafeteria." This "résumé" approach to the college application essay is deadly and altogether unwarranted, since such information will inevitably find an outlet in other sections of the application anyway.

A smarmy voice is a dead giveaway that the writer is deeply worried about not getting into her first-choice college, and so she feels the need to bolster accomplishments whenever and wherever possible. To this I say: *relax*. Settle down and find another tone—an honest, human one that focuses on connecting with the reader rather than impressing the reader. If anything, this is the time to impress the reader with your writing, not with your laundry list of accomplishments.

It's useful, in fact, to think of this essay as a *conversation* you're having with your reader. Imagine yourself at a party. You're sitting on a couch next to someone you don't know. Do you want to be sitting next to someone who's bragging about himself or who is peppering you with silly, slick jokes, or who is tearfully telling you more than you want to know about something? The answer is obviously no. Well, people, that person you're writing to—that admissions counselor—has a lot of the same feelings that you would have and doesn't want to be trapped with a self-important (or self-pitying) bore. So adjust your tone as necessary and be as good and inviting a communicator as you can be.

While there are numerous pitfalls confronting the student writer in this first-draft stage (and we've only touched on a few), let's look at some positive approaches you can use to make this stage of the process more fruitful.

Once More, with Feeling

The very best thing you can do once you've finished your first draft is read it aloud. The ear picks up problems that often escape the eye. Good writing is very much about achieving a satisfying rhythm, not just from sentence to sentence but from paragraph to paragraph and also within the internal structure of each discrete sentence. I like to think of every sentence I write as a wave that builds up momentum as it goes along and then breaks in the spot that feels most natural and right, pulling back out to sea to make way for a new sentence. Further on in this book, we'll examine specific sentences to see why some work and some don't, but for now let's stay with the big picture issues.

You can best hear the internal rhythm of your sentences by speaking each one aloud. This allows you to hear repetitive sentence structures, dull reiteration of words, tangles in which nouns and verbs do not agree, weak passive constructions into which you may have lapsed, and other such common failings. Even though I turn out hundreds of words a day for my work, I still take the time to read those words out loud so that my ear can catch what my eye might miss. I wouldn't know how to do it any other way. In fact, I actually read out loud from hard copy, because I can catch the problems better that way than if I read out loud from a computer screen. But that's just me.

Depending on your living situation, these oral readings of your work can turn into a quasi-public activity, so if you feel it's important to keep your writing tightly under wraps at this stage, you should find a suitably private place. A rooftop, a park bench, the bathroom, your school library, the public library—any of these should do. Then just curl up with your piece and read it out loud, with feeling.

Keep in mind that, for a while at least, every time you go back to read what you've written, you're likely to find more room for improvement. This may be dispiriting at first, but, if you stick with the task, you will likely find yourself accessing the joy of editing. I'm not kidding—there is a certain real pleasure in doing this work and turning flaccid, awkward, dull sentences into tight, smooth, lively ones. Just as there is great pleasure for the silversmith in turning out a ring or for the goldsmith in hammering a sheet of gold, so too there is great satisfaction for the wordsmith in turning out finely crafted sentences and paragraphs.

Draft to Draft

Once you've located your quiet place and have read your essay out loud, you may discover that your first draft simply doesn't work. Let me reassure you: writing is about going from draft to draft until you get it right (not perfect—as I said, there's no such thing as perfection when it comes to writing—but as right as you can make it). The more you get used to editing yourself, the more demanding you'll be and the better your product will become.

The other encouraging bit of news I have to share is that if you stick with the process, you're bound to get results. Whenever I work with a student writer, I usually announce at the very beginning that we'll be going through three or four drafts and a polish before we're through. I have to say that this projection has been dead-on accurate 100 percent of the time. No matter where the student writer starts from on the range of skills—from fairly primitive to a considerable comfort level with writing—the process always seems to fall within this frame.

The first draft is about getting it down on paper. Once it's there, you look it over, shake your head, figure out what works and what doesn't, hold on to what works, and move ahead to the second draft. In the second draft, you might substantially reorganize the chronology of your narrative. Maybe you'll decide to start in the middle and go back to the beginning as the piece progresses. Maybe you'll cut out whole sections that might be colorful or well told but aren't really serving the overall purpose of the essay. Maybe you'll start to wonder why a certain section is there altogether and, as you dig deeper, you'll uncover new layers of meaning.

By the time you reach your third draft, you'll be concentrating on issues of style. Is your voice original, authentic, and compelling? Is your tone too flip or too dry? Are there better ways to say what you're trying to say? Stick with it. Cloister yourself in a silent space. Listen to your voice. If you try hard enough, you're bound to hear those better ways.

Once you've arrived at the final polish stage, you'll be looking at every comma, seeing whether there are any extraneous words to cut, making sure that all your subjects and verbs agree—that sort of thing.

We'll cover these stages in more depth as we go along, but, for now, it's useful to have this overview. Keep in mind, however, that if, at any point in the process, you bail out of one essay and start a new one, the whole process begins all over, and once again you're looking at three or four drafts and a polish.

Working Through the First Draft

Okay—back to the first draft. Where were we? Ah, yes—you found your quiet place, you read your work over, and it was—er, how shall I put this?—not what you had hoped it would be. For starters, you're not sure what the blasted thing is *about*. Well, the problem may be that your piece isn't *about* anything yet. Perhaps the conflict hasn't set in, or maybe you're not even sure what the conflict is.

IDENTIFYING THE CONFLICT

I recently worked with a student named Laura who's a very skilled writer—much more advanced than most students I work with—but her first draft still fell far short of the mark. Laura had been a summer student in a university writing program, and she chose to write about that experience. Her narrative situated her in the university's auditorium, as she waited to go up to the podium to read what she had written. As she sat there, her anxiety escalated until she was practically in a state of palpitation.

Most of Laura's narrative was consumed with details about her pounding heart and sweaty palms. There were also a few rather oblique references to the difficult experiences she had endured over the last few years when she apparently fell out of favor with her high school peer group. In her summer writing program, Laura found a new group of looser, hipper individuals who didn't mind if she sang aloud to the songs of Simon and Garfunkel or danced to the music of Queen. These fellow students had become her true friends, she reflected, as she got up to read . . . and as the piece hurtled toward its indistinct conclusion.

When I conferred with Laura after reading her first draft, I asked her what this piece was *about*. She wasn't sure. Neither was I—but I had a hunch. I guessed that she was layering on the anxiety so thickly, trying to give her piece some kind of heft with all that hyperintense description of pounding hearts and sweaty palms, because she was actually avoiding the other, more significant content that lurked beneath the surface. I sensed that the real conflict had to do with what she had mysteriously alluded to as the experience of being cast outside of her peer group. Immediately, and with almost a tangible sense of relief, Laura told me more about this conflict. In fact, this young woman had been struggling with a serious eating disorder over the course of several years and when word got out among her peers that she was having this problem, she found herself ostracized. The writing program marked the beginning of her journey back into peer group acceptance, reawakening her feelings of trust and friendship.

Once Laura acknowledged the real conflict beneath the surface, she was able to move ahead in her second draft toward a more frank and gritty exploration of her issues. Now I can hear you asking the inevitable questions: Should Laura have even ventured into this subject area? Would it help or hurt her case with admissions officers to expose a history of eating disorders? Frankly, I think there might be a certain element of risk in telling this tale. As I mentioned earlier, eating disorders are such a huge problem at certain institutions of higher learning in this country that an essay of this nature might, in fact, act as something of a red flag for certain admissions counselors. By the same token, an admissions counselor might assume that a prospective student who is up front about this problem is probably well beyond it. More significantly, it is not my place or my job to steer students away from topics they feel driven to write about. I can suggest that a certain line or expression may not present the writer in the best possible light—too negative, perhaps, or too passive or too insensitive—but genuine honesty and a willingness to look deeply at one's history can never be a really counterproductive choice.

DIGGING DEEPER

Because the issue of conflict is so important in this process, let's look at a second example. One of my younger son's best friends is a girl named Eve, whose essay you'll read in the appendix. Eve has a creative sensibility but was never very successful at school. She never found her niche and never really applied herself. When everybody else was sending off their college applications, Eve sat by and watched, planning instead a postgraduate trip to Italy. She intended to spend a few months studying, traveling, and exploring the world beyond the confines of the small town in which she had grown up.

Fortunately, Eve got to enjoy her exciting Continental adventure, but, like all good things, it came to an end. Eventually, it was time to go home, help out in her father's store, and apply to college for the following fall. As Eve had not been a stellar student, she knew her essay was going to count for a lot, so she asked me if I could coach her on it.

At that point, she had already written a first draft. Essentially, it was a pleasant travelogue that took her from Sicily to Florence with maybe a stop in Rome—I don't fully remember. What I do recall is the total absence of any discernible conflict in her narrative. Other than the fact that Eve was writing about Tuscan churches and Sicilian sunsets, her little travelogue wasn't all that different than what I might come up with if I wrote an account describing my usual Saturday morning routine—running errands to the dry cleaner, stopping at Home Depot, and finishing up at

Stop & Shop. Such a narrative would not have had Sicilian sunsets, but it would have been structurally similar—a linear narrative, hopping from place to place, that may have been interesting to me but considerably less so to anyone else reading it.

There was, however, a point in Eve's narrative where she mentioned that her father had come to visit while she was in Florence. Now, one of the best things you can do when moving from your first draft to your second draft is to severely limit the amount of territory you're trying to cover. Eve didn't have a good idea of what to pull out of her travelogue, so I suggested she try to develop something around the story of her father's visit. Being a father myself, and knowing the strains involved in dealing with restless offspring, I had the feeling that some conflict might be lurking in that interaction.

When Eve showed me her second draft, I was struck by an exchange in which her father said to her, "You've run out of money, honey." Eve wrote that she was angry with her father for having said this, and my immediate reaction was "Eureka! Now we have some conflict to work with."

As Eve progressed from draft to draft, she was able to define the conflict and limit her narrative to those actions and situations that served this conflict, penetrating its depths and ultimately resolving it. As her piece evolved—within the customary time frame of three drafts and a polish, as predicted—her father's statement that "You've run out of money, honey" became the inciting action that set off an affecting exploration into Eve's history and her future.

The narrative took us from her father's statement, which he delivered while they sat in a café and which was met with Eve's resentment, to a visit to a museum that she and her father made the next day, during which Eve's anger ebbed and affection for her father resurfaced, to a farewell scene at the airport when it came time for her father to return home. Amid the action of this piece—such as it was, for the action was very subtle, almost transparent—Eve was able to weave her thoughts, questions, and observations.

Eve's narrative, which started out as a mild, diary-like rendition of her trip, evolved into a compelling personal narrative. In it, she confronted the fact that she had never performed to her full potential, acknowledged that she had run out of steam (or "money, honey"), and berated herself for "screwing up once again." But, ultimately, Eve arrived at a place of self-acceptance and qualified optimism, knowing that she would soon be making the trip home and would be facing her future, though with considerably more self-awareness.

The final product struck me as a well-executed and graceful way to address an issue that was lurking beneath the surface of Eve's application: why she had been such an underachiever in high school. Many students who have not excelled in high school feel that they must address that issue in some way in the personal narrative, but I would not necessarily counsel that as a rule. Apologizing for yourself in your college essay can be just as much of a turnoff as shamelessly promoting yourself. If, however, you can address the issue as gracefully as Eve did, then it might be a good way to go. Essentially, you can try it and see how it works. Note the Additional Information section of the Common Application allows you to address academic interruptions, learning issues, and so forth.

What's the Point?

Let's imagine another disappointing first-draft scenario. You've written your piece and you're able to identify some recognizable conflict. But by the time you get to the end of your narrative, something seems to be missing. Could it perhaps be The Point?

It's important to differentiate between the conflict and The Point. You could have plenty of conflict in your narrative. You could be writing about that time you were walking down the street and a gang of kids jumped you, robbing you blind and leaving you in your underwear. But that's just an account of something that happened to you, and bad things happen to everyone. We all get into accidents and lose things and have our failures. What we do with those conflict-ridden incidents—how we resolve them—is The Point. If you've grown from such an incident, if you've done a real turnaround, then that's The Point. And the turnaround doesn't necessarily have to be positive either. It could be an older-but-wiser kind of revelation that you're coming to, as in the case of Jen's story set at Camp Shiloh.

What was The Point of that narrative, anyway? I think it was about staring loss in the face and really feeling the pain that one experiences from such a loss. To me, the implication is that even though Jen feels nothing and fears that she has lost some part of herself at the end of that story, the very act of writing about it suggests that some recovery has been made. And that's The Point— how loss can be absorbed over time and reflection can help remedy loss, even if that reflection is full of pain.

If you think back to the rules of the narrative that I laid out at the beginning of this book, you'll recall that every narrative must convey its "reason to be." There has to be some justification for taking up your reader's precious time—in your case, a very time-poor college admissions counselor who has hundreds of other essays piled up on his or her desk. If The Point of your essay does not come through, then it's going to feel like a time waster to that reader.

If you've written your piece and something in your reading of it or other people's readings of it suggests you've fallen short of your mark, ask yourself whether your point is clear. Why did you even write this story? If you go back to the process I described in Step Two, which explains how you can settle on an essay topic by keeping a list of ideas and noting which ones you keep coming back to, then now is the time to ask yourself *why* you gravitated there. There had to have been a reason.

I'm thinking of a piece by a writer named Ted, who came to me in mid-December with only a few weeks left until his college applications were due. Ted was a bright young man who attended one of the nation's most rigorous preparatory schools, but somehow he had slipped through the cracks of the school's usually expert advising system. His parents were understandably frantic, but he was, shall we say, a bit spaced out.

We had all of one day to pull together his application essay, but fortunately he had managed to get something down on paper in advance of my arrival. He had written a draft of an essay about the weather and, while it was filled with interesting to mildly interesting tidbits about record-breaking hurricanes, tornadoes, and typhoons, what caught my attention were the references of a more personal nature. Ted's friends, for instance, called him "Weatherman." He liked to get up in the middle of the night to watch thunderstorms. These were interesting, eccentric touches that led me to think there was more going on beneath the surface.

Ted did not seem to be in the habit of thinking all that introspectively, so when I asked him why he thought he might be interested in the weather, he couldn't come up with much in the way of an answer. We kept at this line of inquiry, however, and after a while he started to explain that he was fascinated by the weather because it brought home the capriciousness of the universe. The fact that we live in a world where, in a moment's time, a huge wind could blow in and turn everything upside down had a particularly significant resonance for him. As we probed further, we came to a childhood memory in which he was snuggled up in a ski house, warm and secure, while a snow of blizzard-like proportions raged outside. This memory became the kernel of the essay, because what really interested Ted was the idea of holding on to a center in a stormy and sometimes chaotic world. Some of those original tidbits and factoids made the final cut, but the essay had a whole other focus and, most important, a clear point . . . clear enough, that is, to please the admissions folks at Vanderbilt University, where he was admitted.

When you get to appendix 1, you'll find other essays where the digging for The Point became the real focus of the students' work. This digging may also become the focus of your work. Sometimes The Point is right there on the surface; other times, locating it requires some significant excavation. Often, in those cases where such excavation is necessary, The Point is subtle, but this subtlety can make the essay even more powerful and more likely to linger in the mind of the reader.

Moving On

We've talked in this chapter about conflict and point—two areas of your essay that might need to be strengthened. Catching weaknesses isn't easy, and it would be nice to allow your feelings and thoughts about your first draft to bubble up to the surface over a period of time. After all, there's nothing quite like time to lend perspective on a piece of writing. Unfortunately, most students are under too much pressure to enjoy the luxury of such prolonged reflection. In most cases, the student writer will have to jump right into the second draft. So, let's hold our noses and head for the deep end.

Recap

1. You can expect to write three or four drafts and a polish. The first draft is all about getting it down on paper. The second might involve restructuring. The third is often about addressing issues of style. And then comes your final polish.

2. The purpose of writing drafts is to bring vision and execution closer together.

3. Your problem can be related to concept. You tried an idea, and it just didn't work.

4. Maybe the problem is presentation. Your narrative feels too flat, too stilted, overloaded with metaphors, or whatever.

5. Check your structure. Did your piece start abruptly or finish too quickly?

6. How about the tone? Were you maudlin or smarmy, perhaps?

7. Read your first draft aloud and listen for the rhythms . . . or lack of them.

8. Look for the conflict. It's there somewhere.

9. The Point is usually about how we resolve our conflicts.

10. Knowing your point is a way to be respectful of the reader, whose time you never want to waste.

Second Draft

As we've discussed, there's always a certain amount of resistance to overcome when a writer sits down to write, but never more so than when moving from first to second draft. The procrastination that often sets in at the first-draft stage usually has to do with not wanting to face the hard work ahead. The procrastination that accompanies the second-draft stage continues to be about not wanting to do the hard work, but now it's compounded by raw, naked fear.

Am I good enough?

Can I get it right?

I tried and I failed. Why should I believe that next time will be any better?

Okay. It's time to take a deep breath and marshal your forces. You *can* make this work because you *have* to make this work. You're going to concentrate, you're going to focus, you're going to avoid distractions, and you're going to get the job done.

Let's review the situation. Your first draft was just that—a first draft. It was too long and unfocused, spooling out in any number of unrelated directions. You sat down to write, thinking you had a bead on the subject, but it didn't come out nearly as well as you had hoped. In fact, you're not even sure what it's about. And even if *you* know what it's about, you're not sure anybody else will get The Point. So what exactly are you going to do about this?

The answer is you're going to roll up your sleeves and get down to work. After all, what other choice do you have?

Structure and Flow

Now, let's assume that your conflict is relatively clear and you have some sense of The Point of this thing you're writing, but your narrative still isn't quite working. Part of the problem may be that you just haven't told the story very well. Your narrative might be full of extraneous details that get in the way. You know the expression "You can't see the forest for the trees"? In the case of your narrative, maybe you, and the reader, can't see the story for all the details you've piled on. The merit of your story can only really emerge when your *structure* is carefully examined and *flow* is corrected as necessary.

Think back, if you will, to Step One in this book, where we had that story that Mom told. You remember—the one in which she left her purse in the Bed and Bath department of Macy's. Well, maybe you don't remember. After all, it wasn't that memorable. It was a story that had a lot of problems. For one thing, we couldn't really tell what it was *about* because Mom herself, who was telling the story, appeared to be quite uninformed as to the true nature of her conflict. In fact, the true nature of the conflict around that episode of forgetfulness—which, I hypothesized, might have had something to do with her ambivalence about her role as homemaker and mother—was lost in a surfeit of petty and extraneous details. Mom told us that she had run into someone, but that person ultimately had nothing to do with the action of the story. She also told us that the blenders were on sale as well as the bath towels—more irrelevant details. The real heart of her narrative—the vivid thing that we were meant to hold on to, store in our memories, and draw meaning from—was lost in a mass of minutiae. Mom had some structural overhauling to do, if she wanted to make her story flow.

How will you know whether or not your details are extraneous? One way is to have others read your writing, and they may be able to point out what should stay and what should go. But you too will be able to get a feeling for the kind of pruning that needs to be done. Chances are you'll find yourself a bit bored or distracted when you're reading the extraneous details you've included in your narrative, and you'll know it's time to "kill your babies" to improve flow.

In examining your structure, you may decide that you've spent too much time setting things up in the beginning and therefore have too little time to wrap things up at the end, or perhaps too much or too little time in the middle. Usually, these problems are remediable, and you'll become more sensitive to such structural issues as you move from draft to draft. That, in fact, is the business of writing.

Just to take a really simple approach to the assignment, you might think of your narrative as a three-act play . . . or a three-paragraph narrative. Your first paragraph sets up the action and introduces the conflict. The second paragraph plays out the action and examines the conflict. The third paragraph finishes off the action and resolves the conflict. Now there's no reason why you should restrict yourself to three paragraphs, but this is just a way for you to understand how the basic structure works. Three paragraphs = narrative. Each paragraph has and fulfills its purpose.

A structure that has worked really well for my students is the one that I call the "sandwich" (it's actually a kind of triple-decker sandwich). In this structure, you take two actions—a here-and-now "active" action (skiing down a slope, running in a 5K race, knitting, drawing, gardening) and an internal action (like reflecting or reminiscing)—and "sandwich" them together. A writer might start out knitting away on a scarf—*knit one, purl two*—and in the next paragraph pull back to reminisce about how she learned to knit from her grandmother. In the third paragraph, it's back to the action at hand (the knitting), and in the fourth paragraph, the writer goes internal again, reflecting on other things she learned from her grandmother (independence, self-reliance, ethics, whatever). In the fifth paragraph, she holds up the scarf and considers her work.

That's a very simple version of what I'm talking about—though simple can certainly be good. A good thing emerges from this kind of structure: you get a present action that feels narrative, even if not all that much is actually happening, and that acts as a framework upon which to hang the reflective material. If your essay has too much "internal action"—a lot of reflective material that lacks framework—it can seem full of air. By contrast, this "sandwich" approach satisfies the reader's hunger for something more substantial. Also, most people like to read about concrete actions. They learn something new or they identify with what's being described, and that creates a connection.

Just a reminder, while we're on the subject of structure and flow, that first drafts often come in very long. It's not unusual for a writer to get a first draft down in a burst of energy (or a blast of stress), only to discover that the piece clocks in at nine hundred words or more. Yikes! That's considerably longer than the essay is supposed to be. Panic sets in, but there's really no need. Such excess length usually indicates that the writer has taken a circuitous path to his or her destination, but it's perfectly appropriate to wander around at this stage of the game. Once you move on to your second draft, clearer about where you're heading, you can start to hack away at that verbiage.

Radical Surgery

In terms of the big picture editing we're looking at in the second-draft stage, one important strategy is what I call "radical surgery," in which you lop off great portions of your first draft so that you can move more purposefully toward a focused depiction of a smaller piece of time. That kind of surgery is often necessary, for while some students are certainly capable of working with broader themes even in a space as limited as six hundred fifty words, most are not. Six hundred fifty words is really a very small piece of real estate upon which to erect a grand edifice, and chances are you'll find it much easier to build a trim, sturdy cabin on such a small plot of land. But don't worry—a trim, sturdy cabin can have a beauty all its own.

I always encourage my student writers to focus, focus, focus. Sometimes that's hard because you might feel a need to cover a certain amount of time in order to convey a certain amount of growth. What you might discover, however, is that your backstory—that is, your personal history—can be conveyed in just a few strong, well-crafted sentences. Then you'll be freed up to focus on the defining moment that conveys why you set out to write this piece in the first place.

In appendix 1, you'll find an essay by a student named Hannah, whom I mentioned earlier in the book. Hannah had no shortage of conflict to write about. During her senior year of high school, her older sister was suddenly struck with a brain tumor that, for a terrible period of time, threatened to be fatal. Hannah came from a family that was privileged, exuberant, and full of life. In a very real but never obnoxious way, they thought they "had it all"—money, talent, connections—and were profoundly grateful for the wonderful gifts the fates had bestowed upon them. Hannah's sister's health crisis was like a hammer that shattered the shimmering glass bubble they lived in, and while Hannah was terrified by the prospect of losing this beloved sister, she was also desperately and irrationally furious to see the bubble broken.

Hannah was very clear that she wanted to write something about her sister's illness, even though her parents, who were friends of mine, felt that her treatment of the subject, as evidenced by her first-draft attempt, did not bring out Hannah's best qualities. They were right. The Hannah that I read about was unfocused, rambling, and distant. In fact, her first draft felt like a journaling exercise. Now, journaling can be an eminently useful thing to do, but it's not going to get you admitted into the college of your choice. A solid, finished piece, on the other hand, might just do the trick.

Hannah was having a hard time locating the portion of her story that she could pull out and develop into a tight, cohesive narrative, so I suggested she do some more thinking and examination. I posed a question that she could just as well have asked herself. Is there a moment in the entire span of this experience, I wondered, that fills you with particularly intense feelings when you think about it? (I didn't want to pose a question that was too closed because I had no way of knowing at that point whether she was more inclined to write about her fear, her grief, her anger, or what.)

It took Hannah a few days to get back to me with her answer. When she did so, it had to do with an incident that occurred during the summer following her sister's diagnosis. By that time, Hannah already knew that the tumor was benign, so off she went to camp, thinking that the book was closed on this experience. How wrong she was.

At a theater camp for serious young actors, Hannah won the part of Emily in *Our Town*—a classic American play about life and death in an archetypal small town, with Emily acting as the character through whose eyes you watch the drama unfold.

In the story that Hannah told me, she was rehearsing a scene in which Emily is overcome by the piercing reality that mortality always underscores human existence, and in the course of rehearsing that scene, Hannah too was overcome. All the pent-up pain connected to her sister's illness came spilling out, and the result was what the Greeks called *catharsis*.

Catharsis was first defined by Aristotle as the sensation that overcomes the audience at the end of a tragedy. Ultimately, the audience is refreshed by the enlightenment that the tragedy has to offer, and a greater appreciation for life ensues. In modern psychotherapy, *catharsis* has also come to describe the act of giving expression to deep emotions that have never been adequately vented. If your essay can culminate in a true catharsis—your own expression of deep emotions as well as the deep emotions drawn out of your reader—then it stands a good chance of lodging in your reader's memory.

"Well, there's your essay," I remember telling Hannah, once again feeling the little hairs on the back of my neck spring up, and she too was struck by the absolute rightness of it. In fact, it had been her intention to apply for early decision to Brown University, but she essentially abandoned that plan as soon as she started having trouble with her essay. Her divine inspiration—the blazing white flash of recognition that the rehearsal scene *was* the essay—lit a fire under her and literally, in a matter of hours, she produced the powerful essay you'll find in the appendix. She got the application into the overnight mail and some weeks later received her acceptance letter from her college of choice.

Is this a miracle story? In certain ways, it has that quality, particularly with its race-against-time aspect. But that race against time is basically just a dramatic compression of the natural time frame normally required by this process. Hannah simply did what any writer should do: she looked at the entire arc of what she'd written, thought about how she could better convey the conflict, did the most radical surgery of all and essentially abandoned her old essay at the midnight hour in favor of a new one, and thereby found success. Good for her, but one caveat: don't *you* wait for inspiration to strike at the midnight hour. Sure, it can happen, but that's not a great way to live.

Bad Beginnings

When you're thinking about where and how to lop off sections of your overblown nine-hundred-word first draft, there's usually no better place to begin than at the beginning. Invariably, whenever I undertake a writing project—whether it's a short story or an essay or a brochure for a business or a nonprofit organization—I always have the most difficulty with the opening paragraph. It makes sense, because entering a piece of prose is not unlike jumping into a pool of cold water. You have to force yourself to do it, and it might not be a very pleasant sensation at first.

Sometimes I'm actually appalled by how stiff and clumsy my first sentences can be. As I continue writing, my rhythm will pick up, the stiffness will fall away, and the water becomes nice and warm. There's not a thing to do about this process except to go with the flow. Once you reach the end, you can then go back to the beginning in your next draft and knead those doughy opening sentences. Don't get hung up in your first draft with trying to turn these opening sentences, or any of your sentences, into things of beauty. Respect the process of writing drafts and tell yourself that you will improve your product as you move along.

In terms of structure, let's assume that your beginning is a good place to start shearing away excess. Why is that? Well, for one thing, many writers often begin their pieces by saying what they're going to say:

- A most unusual thing happened to me last July 4th.
- I thought I knew what disappointment was until I got a real taste of it when I didn't make the soccer team.
- My definition of friendship changed when I met Jack.

All of these sentences suggest a writer who is rolling up her sleeves, getting ready to do the work. But remember—this step in the process has entirely to do with the writer and nothing to do with the reader. And remember too—there is no room for a prologue in a six-hundred-fifty-word essay.

In an essay of this length, you only have enough time to get into your story, tell it, and get out of your story. Everything else will most likely be material you can—and should—cut. What's more, with sentences like those cited above, you're showing your hand. Why do I even need to read your essay if I know right from the get-go that not making the soccer team was your greatest disappointment? I'm already at the end before I even start out.

There are endless variations of what I'll call the Superfluous Opening. Here are just a few of them:

1. **The Apologetic.**
   I'm not very good when it comes to admitting mistakes, but last summer I really screwed up.

2. **The Sarcastic.**
   You think you've seen craziness? Wait till you hear what happened to me.

3. **The Maudlin.** (Remember that one?)
   Never have I sunk to such despair as the summer I broke my ankle.

4. **The Smarmy.** (Remember that one?)
   For a person of my many achievements, I'd have to say that the one I'm proudest of is my Quiz Bowl performance.

5. **The Overdramatic.**
   I thought I'd seen everything until I reached the rim of the Grand Canyon.

6. **The Been There/Done That.**
   It takes a lot to shock me, but my friend Kim's prom outfit was totally over the top.

Personally, I find every one of these openings to be a turnoff, and if I were a college admissions counselor, I would immediately consign essays with these sorts of openings to piles B, C, and D.

Now, in the case of every one of the writers who wrote the lines above, they ultimately dropped them, thus advancing the action and putting some proverbial pace on the ball. The student who wrote the overly dramatic opening about the Grand Canyon actually took us to the rim and *showed* us—didn't *tell* us—what he wanted us to see. Naturally, his essay was about more than a view of the Grand Canyon, which would be an essay entirely devoid of conflict and, hence, an inadequate essay. He wrote a piece about being burdened in high school, where he felt he had to be perfect at everything, and the sense of proportion he experienced when he arrived at one of Earth's truly awesome spectacles, where he felt blissfully small and imperfect. The student who wrote about his Quiz Bowl performance moved from that smarmy, self-promoting tone to a really funny but insightful piece about how his father rehearsed him relentlessly for the competition and how that kind of pressure made him crazy but also served to bring the two of them closer together.

Egregious Endings

Endings can be just as exasperating as beginnings, sometimes even more so, because some writers will try to cover up inadequacies by overcompensating at the end. That's why it's not unusual to see a construction like this finishing off some essays:

> This truly was one of the most remarkable days I can ever remember having (. . . in my entire life . . . so help me God).

That kind of ending subscribes to the school of thought that says, "If I tell you it was good, then maybe you'll believe me."

The other side of the coin is the ending that just . . . kind of . . . fizzles out. You know what I mean.

> I guess, now that I think about it, it was pretty amazing after all.

And then there's this one:

When I tell people this really happened, they usually don't believe me. Sometimes I'm not sure I even believe it.

That quasi-apologetic way of wrapping things up never really works. Remember that readers don't like to pity a writer. They like a writer to be in command.

Then, of course, there are those essays that just end in the altogether oddest places because the writer has very little understanding of where she's been or how to find the exit door. The only way to resolve such problems is to work hard at understanding the conflict you've chosen to write about. You have to make sure you convey The Point of your narrative (what drew you to this material in the first place) and that you've developed a sturdy scaffold to support your storytelling ambitions.

Keep in mind that with everything we've talked about regarding beginnings and endings, the bottom line is that they are very, very difficult to get right. In fact, I would go so far as to wager that you'll probably spend 30 to 40 percent more time fussing and fiddling with your openings and closings than you will with the rest of your piece. How will you know when you get it right? Your readers will give you feedback, and the most important reader—you—will know it when you get there. There will be that feeling of proportion and rhythm that characterizes good writing. It will be right when it feels right. (And when you read your writing aloud, as I counsel you to do, keep in mind the words of great American composer and musician Duke Ellington, who famously said, "If it sounds good, it is good"). Remember too that I can give you all kinds of advice and even rules, but beyond a certain point, writing is intuitive and you'll have to be the judge.

Playing with Time

When you get to the second-draft stage, you may also want to try playing with time—"playing," that is, in the sense of "manipulating." After all, whoever said time has to be strictly linear, starting at the beginning and moving step by step to the ending?

Feel free to experiment with time however you'd like. See what happens if you start your essay with the ending, for instance. Your essay takes on a reflective tone, doesn't it? As you work your way backward, each event that makes up the narrative will emerge as a piece of the puzzle you hadn't understood when it was happening in its original sequence. By playing with time, you're turning time into a player in your story. If only you'd had more time, if only you hadn't procrastinated, if only you were more organized, then things would have taken a different turn. Time heals all wounds; time wounds all heels.

Now is a good time too to remind you about that tried-and-true literary device called in medias res, or "in the middle of things," which is another way to play with time. A narrative that begins *in the action* might have an opening that sounds like any of the following:

> The elevator lurched.
> The line went dead.
> The door slammed.

Such openings create considerable tension and even excitement. Obviously, by starting an essay this way, you've made the decision not to spend a lot of time setting up the situation, as you would with an opening that sounds like this:

> I was on my way to the periodontist, located on the seventeenth floor of the Metropolitan Building in downtown Cincinnati, when the elevator lurched.

By *not* starting your essay that way, you'll save yourself a lot of room in your six-hundred-fifty-word essay. You may also find that the fact that you were on your way to the periodontist is not all that germane to the point of your story, and the fact that the periodontist was located in downtown Cincinnati is even more irrelevant.

Another interesting way to play with time is to tell your story in *real time*. When you construct a narrative, you will most likely be making a number of quick cuts, such as a filmmaker might make:

> Then we went into his office.
> I left and came back the next day.
> That night I couldn't sleep.

You're making these cuts because you obviously can't tell the reader everything that came in between—like how you ate your grilled cheese sandwich, watched a rerun of *Buffy the Vampire Slayer*, and brushed your teeth. But sometimes a writer may actually want to tell a story from *moment to moment*—as in the hypothetical case of a narrative about being thrown overboard, for instance. From the time you fell out of the boat to the moment when somebody pulled you onto the dock may have taken all of two terrifying minutes. When you tell your story in real time, you're taking us moment by moment through that experience, from beginning to end. Pulling off such a stunt can be very hard, but if you do manage it, you may find that you've written something very gripping that will stick in the mind of your reader.

These are just a few ways you can play with time. Perhaps you'll come up with others. The fact is, there are lots of ways to "play" with writing—that's the joy of it. As you're grappling with beginnings and endings in this second-draft stage and performing the radical surgery that is often necessary, hopefully you'll also begin to feel some of the confidence and pleasure that comes with the stronger writing skills you're developing.

Recap

1. Procrastination problems are often compounded in the second draft by the fear of falling short of one's goal.

2. First drafts often come in very long. Don't panic.

3. A good place to start your "radical surgery" is at the beginning, where often a lot of unnecessary material lurks.

4. Beware of extraneous details, and prune them away relentlessly.

5. Endings often need a lot of extra attention, because they tend to overcompensate or trail off.

6. You may also want to consider "playing with time." Manipulating the chronology of your narrative or starting in the middle of things can be effective strategies.

STEP SEVEN

Self-Editing

By the time you finish your second draft, you should have a good sense of whether or not your essay is a keeper. Most likely, at this point, you will have completed your major structural work. In essence, you will have framed out your house, and if things are looking fairly plumb, then you should be able to move ahead confidently with your construction plans. On the other hand, if you're feeling like your house might blow down in a strong wind, then you must realize, sad as that may be, that now is not the time to hang the shutters and string the Christmas lights. Believe me—you have my sympathy. I've been there often, and I know how hard it can be to throw in the towel on something you've labored over. Getting stuck in denial mode is just a form of procrastination, however, and the time you spend in that place could be put to better use getting a new narrative under way.

For the purposes of this chapter, let's assume that the structure of your piece is falling into place; the conflict feels sharp and defined; the proportions make sense (that is, you're not spending three-quarters of the allotted space describing the first quarter of the action); and your point, if not yet crystallized, is at least glimmering. So now that things are perking along, let's take a look at some issues of style.

Edit Thyself

As you must surely realize, you've been editing yourself all along during the course of this assignment. As you've developed your ability to self-edit, you've been able to judge your performance on the "big picture" elements of your essay—where it's strong, where it falls down, where it gets fuzzy, and so on. The ability to self-edit is absolutely central to your development as a writer. Even if you were to receive a great deal of input from your English teacher, or if you had a coach like me to provide you with input, or, heaven forbid, if you paid someone to write your essay for you, you would still have to come to that same place that every writer must reach: a place of real ownership of your work. Until you can claim that sense of ownership, your piece will not reflect your authentic voice.

Your *authentic voice* is that part of you—like your eyes, your voice, or your thumbprint—that expresses your individuality. And, as we discussed, the personal narrative is the designated place to let that individuality shine through. That's why the personal narrative plays such an important part in the college application process. It's your opportunity to differentiate yourself from everyone else.

By the time you reach Step Seven of this process, you should be ready to stamp your material with your own personal *style*. A lot goes into the development of a writing style, so read on for some useful insights.

Metaphors: The Well-Dressed Essay

If we think of the narrative as an outfit, let's imagine metaphors as the jewelry—bright, shiny things that attract attention. Most people enjoy jewelry, but if you were to consult with an employment counselor who was sending you out on a job interview, she might explain that, when you dress to make a good impression, your best approach to the issue of jewelry is to go easy on the shiny stuff. She would advise you not to show up with gigantic hoop earrings or sparkly spangles or charm bracelets that herald your arrival. A lot of people don't like that look, and your goal, when you're going for a job interview, is to follow the path of least resistance. Why engage in high-risk behavior, like wearing ankle bracelets or mood rings, that some people, fairly or unfairly, might deem just a tad tacky? Similarly, why clutter up your narrative with too many metaphors? It will just distract your reader from your work.

CLICHÉS AND OTHER "METAPHOR MISTAKES"

A good *rule of thumb* (cliché) regarding metaphors is that if they sound as if you've heard them before, don't use them. The likelihood is that they're clichés. Just to make sure we're all *on the same page* (cliché), let's define a cliché as a terminally tired expression that *has been around the block too many times* (cliché) and is ready to be *retired to the farm* (cliché). Clichés immediately telegraph a stunning lack of imagination—which is exactly what you don't want to convey to a college admissions counselor. In a great many instances, clichés are metaphors or similes—simply stale ones: *Like a bat out of hell. Like a rolling stone. Like water off a duck's back.* These similes are so familiar that they fail to have any new meaning for us.

Sometimes it can be fun to use clichés if you're interested in things like slang and idiomatic speech, which I am. (And which may explain why you'll find the occasional—at least I *hope* occasional—cliché in this text.) If you're a fiction writer, you may want to depict a character who spouts clichés, and, of course, such people do exist and have a place—usually a comic one—in literature. But unless you're depicting such a character in your application essay for some reason—perhaps a parody of a teacher, let's say—you should do your best to avoid clichés altogether.

One more word of caution while we're on the subject of clichés—sometimes they're so thick in the prevailing culture that you can't even hear them and tend to easily *buy into them* (cliché). Think about the expressions you hear all over the place these days—*thinking outside the box, putting in the sweat equity, knocking one out of the park, a win-win situation.* How many of these clichés do you use in your daily speech? Just because something is present in the media and might sound hip and cool doesn't mean it isn't a cliché. Far from it.

What does an original metaphor sound like? Here's one from a poem called "Coyote Wind" by Ohio poet Imogene Bolls:

Scratching at the window with claws of pine, the wind wants in.

The wind with claws of pine—now that's an arresting image. Its utter originality makes you sit up and take notice. It creates a picture in your mind. If your metaphor doesn't do that, then don't bother with it.

One way to misuse metaphors is to mix them up in odd, discordant ways. Generally speaking, mixed metaphors will bring down the level of your work. Consider this example taken from an essay by a writer I'll call "Devon":

My grandfather had the sleek bone structure of an eagle with flinty eyes and a rosy glow.

Devon was so insistent about wanting us to see what his grandfather looked like—as if such physical details even count for much in an essay of this length—that he made the mistake of mixing his metaphors. He used animal (eagle), vegetable matter (rose), and mineral (flint) references—none of which go together very well. In his urgency to make us see, he didn't even allow us to get a good look. And Devon didn't just mix his metaphors, but he also piled them on. That is hardly the best way to use them.

Proportion and Rhythm

If we continue to think of the narrative as an outfit, then before we even start putting on the jewelry (that is, the metaphors), we should pay attention to more important wardrobe issues, like proportion, for instance. Does the length of your jacket go with the length of your pants? An overly long jacket combined with an overly short pair of pants can quickly make you look like a Barnum & Bailey clown. Cast a critical eye on the proportions of your narrative and see whether things are as they should be.

In the last step, we talked about not letting your opening occupy a disproportionate amount of time. Does it? Do you find yourself rushing to finish your story? Or do you perhaps have a skimpy opening, a tacked-on ending, and a big, potbellied middle section that feels like it's taking forever to get through? (Believe it or not, a six-hundred-fifty-word essay *can* feel like forever.)

Check too to make sure that your individual sentences are not disproportionate. It's good to vary sentence lengths, but you must do so with a sense of rhythm. How can you determine whether your piece has rhythm? How else? By reading it aloud. (*If it sounds good, it is good.*) You will be able to hear whether there is a flow or not and whether, for instance, a staccato section is there for a reason—crisp and abrupt, to convey a distinct mood, perhaps of tension or anxiety—or is present simply because your writing is choppy. And remember too that punctuation is another critical factor in establishing rhythm. Every comma you put in or take out affects the rhythm of your piece. A misplaced comma can stop the action in exactly the wrong place. I cannot provide a guide to punctuation in this slim volume, but you'll want to make sure that you have a good understanding of punctuation and/or that your piece will be proofread by someone who has a good understanding of punctuation.

Tone

Sticking with our metaphor, tone is the color, the texture, and the cut of your outfit. Some people favor clothing in shades of sulfurous yellow, shocking pink, and screaming lime green. To that, I say, leave it at home. You're going on an interview, remember? This is not the time for loud colors, cutouts, pom-poms, leather appliqués, or embroidered images of bucking broncos. And, when it comes to your college essay, this is not the time either for linguistic lapses in tone. So let's see how we can control tone in order to create a pleasing and harmonious piece of writing.

TUNING UP YOUR TONE

There are quite a few ways in which your tone can go awry at this stage of the process. Remember Step Five and an earlier draft, when I cautioned you on tone. We identified the stuffy, sarcastic, maudlin, and smarmy voices as being serious lapses in tone. These lapses may be lingering in your latest draft, so beware of them. You may be overly intense about making your point:

> It was the most unbelievable, incredible, outrageous night of my life.

Or that smarmy, self-serving thing might still be hanging around:

> In all modesty, few people have achieved as much in the position of student government leader as I have.

You might sound lackluster, depressed, strung out—which is often evidenced by an overreliance on qualifiers:

> I kind of think that my trip to New Orleans was, in a way, sort of a breakthrough in the quest for what you might call my real identity.

Or you might not have weeded out that flip, breezy, chatty, cutesy thing:

> I don't know why but trouble, with a capital "T," sticks to me like cat hair to velour pants.

Yikes! Give it a rest, will ya, buddy?

At this point in the process, when writers—and not just inexperienced ones—are often afflicted with a bad case of nerves, the best thing you can do for yourself is take a deep breath, slow things up, and, in as calm and collected a way as possible, just try to get your story down on paper. Once you get a tone you feel comfortable with, things will flow much more smoothly.

Authentic Voice

Let's remember that you're striving here to capture your authentic voice. You have one—you use it all the time—but you may not be getting a hold of it in your writing. For the sake of this discussion, let's split the tone issue down the line, between "formal" on one side and "informal" on the other. Your goal is to stay somewhere in the spacious middle. "But I'm not a middle-of-the-road person," you say. No problem. In the vast majority of life's circumstances, you can gravitate to your favored pole, but not just now; if you don't mind, let's stay on more neutral ground.

Once again, you have to keep in mind who you're writing for, which is exactly what I do when I'm creating marketing materials for my higher-education clients. Colleges and universities often hire me to write recruitment materials that are aimed at eighteen- to twenty-one-year-olds. I keep that market firmly in mind as I write. I don't try to write down to this audience— *Hey, bro, the dining hall is da bomb*—but I do try to maintain an engaging conversational tone. These higher-education clients will also hire me to write fund-raising materials, which are aimed at potential donors, most often alumni in their fifties, sixties, and seventies. Here, the school wants to project an image of dignity that will persuade someone to make a nice gift in their behalf. Consequently, in such situations, I write copy that is measured and dignified, but that I try to enliven with good, solid, muscular prose. The point is that in these situations, as with most every situation in which I find myself as a writer, I must keep my audience in mind, and I'm suggesting you do the same.

We've established who your audience is—the overworked college admissions counselor who has already seen a slew of essays before yours rises to the top of the pile. This poor reader has been subjected to blowhards who tout their achievements way out of proportion, dullards who drone on about a whole lot of nothing, and show-offs who try to dazzle with fancy words. What this reader is really longing for is a writer with an *authentic voice*. A writer who seems genuine and original will very likely make a significant impact on this poor jaded reader.

In trying to stay somewhere in the middle in terms of tone so that you won't distract your reader with excessive formality or informality, you should understand the features that can convey those respective qualities. Let's start with formality.

FORMALITY

Formality has its place at coronations, papal investitures, and other such stately events, but, as a rule, a formal tone does not speak very compellingly to the average person. In fact, if you were to poll a group of people on the characteristics they associate with formality, you'd probably hear such descriptors as "stuffy," "snobby," "cold," and "stiff." Very few young people who are applying to college these days are actually formal in nature, but that doesn't mean I don't see a lot of formal writing. Why is that? Well, many of these young men and women equate "formal" writing with "good" writing. They approach an important writing assignment, such as the college application essay, as they would a fancy sit-down dinner. Which fork should they use for the shrimp cocktail? Does the napkin go on the lap or under the chin? They get so hung up on the rules of writing that they forget what's really important: to find and use your authentic voice.

Let me give you an example of what I'm talking about. Some people have been taught that it is highly incorrect to end a sentence with a preposition. So instead of writing something like this:

> He showed her how to use the exercise ball to stretch, which is what it was designed for.

they'll write something like this:

> He showed her how to stretch with the exercise ball, for which use, the ball was designed.

Okay, gang, here's the scoop on prepositions: it's entirely kosher to end a sentence with one. Yes, there may be some admissions counselors who are still laboring under the impression that this practice is incorrect, but chances are that even those individuals will be far more persuaded by a sentence that falls clearly and naturally on a preposition than one that gets all tangled up trying to avoid such a terrible fate. As far as I'm concerned, the final word on this nonsense was sounded years ago by British prime minister Winston Churchill, who, when asked what he thought of ending a sentence with a preposition, wittily declared, "This is the sort of English up with which I shall not put."

Another thing I often see from my student writers that makes their work sound stiff is the use of the phrase *to be*. I'm talking about constructions like these:

- I found it to be a very interesting film.
- I would like there to be more communication in the Student Senate.
- To protect the environment, it would be better for there to be more government regulation.

Each of those stiff sentences could easily be rewritten in a way that would save precious words and would save the reader precious time plowing through such bulky constructions. Consider these rewrites:

- This film was very interesting.
- The Student Senate needs more communication.
- More government regulation would help protect the environment.

Now aren't these excellent examples of that dictum I shared with you at the beginning: *less is more?*

Another way that your writing can take on a formal, stuffy tone is when you lapse into the passive voice. The difference between the active voice and the passive voice is that in the situation of the active voice, somebody or something performs the action, whereas in a passive voice situation, the action is being done *to* somebody or something. Consider these examples:

Active: The batter hit the ball over the fence.
Passive: The ball was sent over the fence by the batter.

Active: Jack and Mary adopted a dog from the pound.
Passive: A dog was adopted from the pound by Mary.

Active: Ambassador Hopkins accepted the award.
Passive: The award was accepted by Ambassador Hopkins.

Reading these examples, you'd think it was totally natural and almost inevitable that a writer would select the active voice every time, but you'd be surprised how often we opt for the passive voice instead. Why is that? Perhaps there's a psychological reason. A lot of people feel insecure when it comes to writing, and they unconsciously choose the passive voice, which reflects their timidity.

Is the passive voice ever justified? Maybe when it comes to literary fiction. A writer might be creating a character who likes to have things done to him rather than doing things himself. Maybe the character is bored or shy, lacks motivation, or whatever. In a sense then, using the passive voice to underscore character is analogous to using clichés to underscore character. In either case, it is doubtful that such a situation will arise in your essay. But, hey—you never know.

INFORMALITY

Just as we don't want to be overly formal, neither do we wish to sound too informal. Getting back to the controlling metaphor of this chapter, the college application essay is something of a dress-up occasion and you don't want to show up in cutoffs and a tank top. You don't want to wear a tuxedo either, but at least you should be in a clean, pressed shirt and a decent pair of slacks or skirt.

What does "too informal" sound like?

For one thing, there's a lot of slang—what one might call the language of the day. Stuff like:

- I was chillin' with my friends when a car pulled up.
- Yo, those shoes are so ghetto.
- Jen came down the stairs, looking so hot.

This is neither the time nor the place, bro, to be chillin' with the homies. This is the time to clean up your act and write in a style that any reader can appreciate.

But, you may be thinking, what about that authentic voice you keep talking about?

Good question—and here's your answer. Why do you assume that your "chillin' with the homies" voice is your *authentic* voice? Maybe it's just a hat you're trying on for the moment. If you take the hat off—and rest the street talk for a bit—you may actually hear your authentic voice coming through.

It's important at this point to distinguish between formal and serious, or informal and lighthearted. You can write about serious issues without sounding like you're the Chancellor of the Exchequer or whatever. Similarly, you can write a lighthearted piece—let's say a warmly comic portrayal of life lessons you learned from your eccentric Uncle Jack, the inventor—but it needn't be the equivalent of a stand-up routine, full of scatological jokes and hey-look-at-me kind of language.

No matter what situation we're talking about—serious, lighthearted, sad, joyous, angry, satirical, romantic, disillusioned—you're still going to be looking for a tone that rests somewhere in the middle between formal and informal. But middle-of-the-road in this instance doesn't have to mean bland.

The issues we've been talking about—proportion, rhythm, tone, and voice—all require your focused attention. You want your narrative to look its best. Now we'll move on to the third draft, where you'll be refining your sensitivity to language ever further.

Recap

1. Your authentic voice is that part of you that expresses your individuality in your writing.

2. Keep an eye out for mixed metaphors and eliminate them from your writing.

3. If a metaphor sounds like something you've heard before, don't use it. It's probably a cliché.

4. Beware of supposedly hip, current expressions you hear in the media. By the time you use them in your writing, they may already have turned into clichés.

5. Read your piece for proportion and rhythm, and remember that punctuation affects rhythm.

6. Continue to check your narrative for tone, avoiding the stuffy, smarmy, maudlin, and sarcastic.

7. Find a middle ground between a formal and an informal tone.

Third Draft

As you move your essay along to the third-draft stage, you should be feeling relatively confident. Hopefully, by now, every time you read your essay, you're hearing something of that deep, resonant *thwack* like the one you get when you hit the "sweet spot" on your tennis racket. The structure should be in place and the conflict should feel juicy. But, at the same time, you recognize there's still work to be done. Let's think metaphorically again. You've created a sculpture that clearly has some great lines and a dynamic sense of movement, but there are lumps and rough patches waiting to be smoothed out and cleaned up in some fashion. The work ahead is not overwhelming, but that's not to say it's easy.

At this point, to finish off the job, you'll need to draw on all your sensitivity to language. Once again, I recommend reading your work out loud. (*If it sounds good, it* is *good.*) Many of us have enough musical intelligence to be able to hear when a singer is flat. We're not necessarily musicians, but, as practiced listeners, we can pick up on mistakes. Unfortunately, in our culture, few people use their iPods to listen to the written word, and so our ears are not as attuned to hearing mistakes in prose. That doesn't mean, however, that you can't become more attuned—you just have to work at it. Retreat to a quiet spot, read your essay out loud, and do your best to hear when your prose gets thick, when it gets dull, and when you lose your way.

To help with this task, I'm going to provide you with some necessary tips and pointers. But, before we continue, let's just spend a moment recalling the bad habits I cautioned you against in the last chapter, like slipping into the passive voice and overusing and mixing metaphors. You're still going to want to keep an eye out to make sure such problems don't linger into this third-draft stage, but now it's time to pay close attention to some other style issues as well.

Keep It Clean

I keep coming back to that phrase so closely associated with modern design: *less is more*. That famous dictum was a reaction to the design precepts of the Victorian, Edwardian, and French Empire eras. According to those precepts, a sitting room was not considered proper unless there were doilies on the overstuffed chairs, tassels on every drape, beaded shades on every lamp, and urns, vases, and statuary adorning every surface. The design principles that followed, based on clean lines and natural textures and light, felt like a breath of fresh air. Your essay, following the dictum *less is more*, can also provide fresh air for the weary admissions counselor who has been sloughing his way through a pile of overstuffed essays. He's about had it with all that thesaurus-driven language and excessive use of adverbs and adjectives. When some clean, graceful prose comes along, the effect is nothing less than bracing. But how do you achieve such prose? Again, the idea is to go easy on the metaphors, stick with the active voice, and keep certain pointers in mind—such as avoiding exclamation points.

Some writers are inordinately fond of exclamation points and will use them indiscriminately. Although the exclamation point has an appropriate function in the English language—as when a character yells "Fire!" or "Help!" or "Stop, thief!"—it should be assiduously avoided in almost all other contexts.

Writers who pepper their work with exclamation points—*It was such a fun day! I never saw anything like it! Tina was the best friend a girl could have!*—are trying to enliven their limp prose with a desperate perkiness. In that respect, the exclamation point represents one small step up the evolutionary scale from the "i" that is dotted with a smiley face. Is it necessary to add that the double exclamation point—*It was such a fun day!!*—only compounds this transgression? Cardinal rule: Double exclamation points are only to be used by comic strip writers who also favor such constructions as !!Ø#!! to convey a very bad day.

Adverb Abuse

Like exclamation points, adverbs play an appropriate role in the English language, but they are also too often misused. Here are some examples of adverbs that are used appropriately:

- The thief moved silently through the room.
- The audience laughed uproariously at the clown.
- The dancer moved gracefully across the stage.

Even though these adverbs may be used correctly, they don't make for particularly exciting writing. It would be better to find a strong verb to take the place of these adverbial constructions—for example, the dancer glided across the stage or the audience shrieked with laughter. More about strong verbs in a moment, however.

Back in the 1930s, a series of science fiction novels for young adults was published with a main character named Tom Swift. These exuberant little volumes were characterized by a peculiar reliance on adverbs, creating sentences that came to be known as "Tom Swiftisms." These absurd constructions sounded like this:

- "My horse came in!" he said winningly.
- "Don't mess with Othello," the Moor said darkly.
- "I've struck oil," Tom said crudely.

It takes some imagination—though not a great deal—to come up with such adverbial absurdities, and we'll assume your essay is free of such extremes. But you might still be overdosing on adverbs, thereby clogging up your writing.

I see a lot of essays with sentences like these:

- My brother lurked furtively by the door.
- Jen giggled foolishly over her little joke.
- Mrs. Murray glared witheringly at me.

Consider those examples and ask yourself whether the adverbs serve any purpose. After all, can you really "lurk" in a way that's not "furtive"? Doesn't "giggling" imply a certain foolishness? Have you ever seen a "glare" that wasn't "withering"?

I think not.

The Human Voice

When it comes to enlivening your essay, dialogue can be one of your most effective tools. Good dialogue virtually leaps off the page—which is why you don't want to bring it down for a crash landing with awkward adverbial constructions like "she said cheerfully" or "he sneered menacingly."

One way to look at dialogue is as a spice that will enhance this stew you're cooking. You started with onions, garlic, tomatoes, and meat bones, and you cooked it all down until you got something rich and complex. Now you're going to add the snippets of spice or herbs to bring out even more flavor. If you're at all familiar with cooking, you know that you want to use a light hand when it comes to adding your curry powder, cayenne pepper, or tarragon. The same holds true for dialogue. Dialogue is not there to provide exposition—"Lift the hood, Sam, and see whether the fan belt is running as it should because, if not, we're going to have to take the car into the shop." Snooze. That kind of information is best dispatched in as few brief sentences as possible. Dialogue is best reserved for moments like, "Darn! The fan belt's gone!" Sam said. That's the kind of moment that will hold your reader's attention.

In general, keep your dialogue short and punchy. Use dialogue when you want to introduce interesting new developments into the narrative. Dialogue along the lines of "Good morning, Mrs. Jones. Lovely day, isn't it?" is as deadly on the page as it can be in real life. Also, when you're writing dialogue, think about the person who's speaking it. Each of us has a distinctive voice. If your science teacher speaks a line of dialogue in your story, it shouldn't sound the same as a line of dialogue from your friend T. J. or from your grandmother or from your little brother. To write dialogue that will work, you have to inhabit the characters that speak the lines. And, as a general rule, if you don't feel that you can pull off dialogue, then don't do it. No dialogue is far better than bad dialogue.

Crime novelist Elmore Leonard, widely recognized as one of the supreme stylists in the field of contemporary fiction and author of books that were the basis for such films as *Get Shorty,*

Out of Sight, and *Jackie Brown*, counsels against using any word other than "said" to carry a line of dialogue. "The line of dialogue belongs to the character," Leonard says. "The verb is the writer sticking his nose in."

By Leonard's standards, "Don't do it," Josh pleaded or "Don't do it," Josh whined or "Don't do it," Josh wheedled are all less effective than "Don't do it," Josh said. I concede Leonard's point, but, for our purposes, if you were to write, "Don't do it," Josh whispered or "Don't do it," Josh cautioned, I doubt you'd find an admissions counselor in the country who would hold it against you.

But Leonard does make another point relevant to the college application essay. He says, "Never use an adverb to modify the word 'said.'" In other words, "Jack said wisely" is a far less effective piece of writing than simply "Jack said."

Don't Waste Time

Earlier in this book, I pointed out that the relationship between writer and reader is a structured one, almost a contract of sorts. One aspect of that contract is the implicit understanding that some kind of point is going to be made—as subtle as that point may be. Another aspect of the contract is the agreement that you're not going to deliberately waste your reader's time. Now, you may ask, "What if I've written about Etruscan vases and my reader simply isn't interested in Etruscan vases? Have I wasted that reader's time?" That's a good question, to which I would reply, "Of course you haven't. The reader is always within her rights to put down a piece of writing that doesn't interest her and move on to the next reading experience. You've done nothing wrong." In terms of waste, I'm referring to those words that use up precious seconds of your reader's time. There should be absolutely no waste in your writing. Every word—every comma—should be there for a reason. In the section on overuse of adverbs, we were essentially dealing with a time-wasting issue. It takes additional time—precious seconds—to read "lurked furtively" instead of just "lurked," or "glared witheringly" instead of "glared."

Oh, come on, I can hear you saying. We're talking about maybe a nanosecond. Give me a break.

Sorry—but I'm serious. The basic precept against wasting time that underlines the contract is still in force, whether we're talking about a nanosecond or a thousand nanoseconds.

Find Strong Verbs

One of the rewarding things about writing is that you have countless words at your disposal. Finding and using strong verbs will not only strengthen your writing, but it will also save precious time for your reader. First of all, a good verb will go a long way toward resolving the problem of adverb abuse. As I mentioned above, "lurking" implies something furtive and "glaring" implies something withering, so you don't need those pesky adverbs going along for the ride. Look at these two ways of saying the same thing:

> Jim hung around the sidelines in a suspicious and resentful manner, casting unpleasant glances at Pete, who had taken his place in the lineup.

Another way of saying that is

> Jim lurked on the sidelines, glaring at Pete, who had taken his place in the lineup.

And the winner is . . . the second version, which is forceful and to the point. So do your homework and find the verb that can rid you of all those extra words. Instead of describing someone as "sitting restlessly," use the verb "fidget." Instead of "sitting around gloomily"—as if "gloomily" is a word that anyone would really feel comfortable using or reading—substitute the word "mope." Do you want to describe someone who "takes enormous delight in swing dancing"? How about saying that such a person "revels" in swing dancing? And when you do find strong verbs, don't undermine your good work by then attaching meaningless modifiers to them, as in

- He sort of lurked.
- He kind of lurked.
- He seemed to lurk.

Those extra words just telegraph your insecurity. And, by the way, this is one of those instances where some thesaurus research is justified. If you look up the word "enjoy," you might discover "revel." Just be careful not to use some phrase like "luxuriate in" that your thesaurus might suggest but that would sound very strange in conjunction with swing dancing. As good writing practice in general, you might start keeping a list of verbs you discover, storing them away for future use. You never know when you might want to pull out a "gambol" or a "gyrate" or a "gravitate."

AVOID REPETITION

While we're on the subject of good fresh words versus dull stale ones, let me also point out the importance of avoiding word repetition. I'll do almost anything not to use the same word more than once in a sentence, or even from sentence to sentence. I'm not talking about "if," "and," or "but," obviously, but I really don't like this sort of thing:

Jim couldn't face the consequences of his actions. The idea of facing his parents after crashing up the car was more than he could bear.

To my way of thinking, when a writer repeats a word like "face" (or "facing"—just a variation of the same verb), it suggests a certain bankruptcy of imagination or simply an I-don't-care attitude. As a writer, I'll always work a little harder to avoid that trap and will write something like this instead:

> Jim couldn't deal with the consequences of his actions. The idea of facing his parents after crashing up the car was more than he could bear.

Don't run the risk of boring your reader.

Question Your Adjectives

Having already denounced unnecessary adverbs, I'll give equal time to adjectives that serve little, if any, purpose. Here's an example of prose written with a heavy reliance on adjectives as well as adverbs:

> The old dog, grayed at the muzzle, with yellow teeth and cloudy eyes, sat stiffly by his water bowl, bending over with great difficulty to lick his grizzled paw. His pained expression suggested that he was having a particularly bad day with his severe arthritis.

Now let's try that without the adjectives but with some strong verbs instead:

> The old dog, seated by his water bowl, strained to give his paw a lick. He groaned. It was a bad arthritis day.

Which do you prefer? Let me guess. You prefer the one with fewer words. Not only does it require less time to read the thing, but there's also a spare, simple grace that allows you to conjure up an image more easily than the longer version, which tries to *supply* the image. A good writer doesn't feel compelled to do the reader's work. A good writer recognizes the implicit collaboration in the writing-reading relationship, in which both parties have a role to play, and so doesn't color in every picture and explain every action, every relationship, and every nuance of the story. A good writer is respectful of the *mind's eye*—that plane of consciousness upon which the reader can bring to bear his own associations and references.

Ask yourself this question: Are your adjectives making your picture clearer and more vivid, or are they just getting in the way? Let me share with you some good writing I've recently encountered in a novel called *The Moviegoer* by Walker Percy. This novel, first published in 1962 and the winner of the National Book Award, follows a young man in New Orleans as he moves about his seemingly conventional and comfortable life in search of something meaningful. The writing is consistently fresh and original. Here is the hero as he sits sandwiched on a train between his girlfriend and a stranger who is sleeping:

> My head, nodding like a daffodil, falls a good three inches toward the St. Louisan before it jerks itself up. Kate sits shivering against me, but the St. Louisan is as warm and solid as roast beef.

In those two sentences, there are two similes—his head is *like a daffodil* and the St. Louisan is as warm and solid *as roast beef.* In a twinkle, those similes say a great deal more about this character—a fanciful, questing man-boy—than a lot of adjectives like "fanciful" or "questing" would accomplish. The worst kind of writing occurs when the writer obviously resorts to the temptations of the thesaurus in his hunt for adjectives. He wants to describe an elderly man, and the word *elderly* in the thesaurus leads him to *aged,* which in turn offers such alternative choices as *venerable, doddering, senescent*, and *hoary*. Hmmh, The Writer thinks. *Hoary.* Now there's a word you don't see coming and going. So The Writer writes:

> The hoary teacher, so experienced in the classroom, illuminated his young students with his wisdom.

The Writer sits back, pleased with himself. Little does he know that the word *hoary* has certain specific nuances and connotations, as almost all words do, and the use of the word in this context sounds exceedingly peculiar. Yes, if you were to look up *hoary* in the dictionary you might see the definition "ancient," but you'd also see "white or grayish white, as from age." And even if you wanted to signify that the teacher was white or grayish white, as from age, you should still know that the word *hoary*, used as an adjective, has been out of favor for probably 150 years. Silas Marner might have been hoary. Your math teacher, in the twenty-first century, is most likely not, and don't let any thesaurus trick you into thinking he is.

Lost and Found

Many writers waste their reader's time by losing their way and forcing the reader to untangle sentences that have gotten all knotted up. Sometimes when I'm editing a student's paper, it can take me entire *minutes* to untangle a badly snarled sentence. I don't mind it so much—after all, I'm getting paid for my time—but don't expect a college admissions counselor to feel the same. She's going to feel just as frustrated as you do when the garden hose is all tangled up, and she's going to simply toss that essay onto the reject pile and turn to a new one that doesn't require her to do double duty.

Here's an example of the kind of sentence I often come up against:

> On the way to the bank, not knowing that he had a hole in his pocket, John's money fell out which he only realized when he got to the front of the line.

This is such a difficult sentence to fix that it's hard to know where to start, but it certainly would help to understand that the two absolutely essential components of any sentence are the subject and the verb. It would be nice to think that everyone understood this by the time they reached their last year of high school and were applying to college, but you'd be surprised.

Simply put, a sentence is not a sentence unless it has (a) a subject and (b) a verb. Otherwise put, a sentence has to have an action (the verb) and somebody or something that performs the action (the subject). *I sit* is a perfectly legitimate sentence. *Sit down* is not—unless it is a command, with (*you*) as the implied subject. *Philosophy sucks* is a sentence—although not one we'd want to see in your college essay. But, even so, the sentence has an action—*sucking*—and there is a thing, *philosophy*, performing the action.

We don't have the time or space in this book to explore the art of sentence structure, as much as I might like to. It would be good for you to fully understand what makes a compound sentence, a complex sentence, and so forth. It is useful to know that a compound subject is one that has two individuals or things performing the action—*Jack and Jill went up a hill; hot dogs and sushi make you thirsty*—while a compound verb represents two or more actions, as in *Jack and Jill ran and skipped down the street* or *Playing golf can delight or frustrate you.* When we have a good grasp on sentence structure, we can avoid some nasty tangles. Ask your English teacher for extra help with sentence structure if you feel less than confident about your abilities in that department, but, for now, let's try to stick with a general rule: place your subject and verb as close to the beginning of the sentence as possible and build out from there. Following that rule is a good way to avoid getting lost.

Consider the problematic sentence cited—the one about losing money before John got to the bank—and see how much clearer it becomes when subject and verb start off the sentence:

> John lost his money on the way to the bank, not realizing until he got to the front of the line at the teller's window that he had a hole in his pocket.

You can feel much more confident about building your sentences up with additional clauses as long as you have your subject and verb at the beginning. When you get to be a really expert writer, you can play around with that rule if you choose, but, for now, adhering to it will help keep you out of trouble.

Vague Reference

Another excellent way to get lost in a sentence is to fall into the trap of vague reference. Vague reference can often pose problems in sentences that include such words as "this," "it," and "which." The writer uses such pronouns, but doesn't make it clear what those pronouns refer back to. For instance:

> I went to the country, got a bad case of poison ivy, got lost on the way home, and had a flat tire, which is why I didn't get back to work on time.

What does the "which" in that sentence refer to? It should refer to one item, but we have no idea which one.

I often see another kind of mistake connected to vague reference, where a student will write something like this:

In our high school handbook, it says that students are not permitted to smoke.

What is the "it" in this sentence? Is it the handbook? The administration? It would be so much simpler to say this:

Our high school handbook says [or states] that students are not permitted to smoke.

Another example of vague reference is one that's ambiguous because it's not clear which party the pronoun refers to:

Most teenagers can coexist peacefully with their parents as long as they are treated with respect.

As long as who is treated with respect? The teens or the parents? We have no way to answer that question based on the use of the pronoun "they" in this context. To convey the desired meaning, you would have to rephrase the sentence along these lines:

As long as teenagers are treated with respect, they can coexist peacefully with their parents.

Eliminating vague reference will help a great deal in forming better, stronger sentences.

Put Some Pace on It

The great benefit to understanding sentence structure is that you can then experiment with it, creating sentences that vary in rhythm and putting some pace on your piece. Here's an example of a paragraph that has nothing going on in the way of pace:

> I went to Harvard summer school last year. I studied anthropology. I discovered that people are very much the same all over the world in spite of surface differences.

Now let's spin it another way:

> Last summer, I studied at Harvard. I signed up for anthropology, not quite sure what to expect, but, over the course of the summer, I made an important discovery. People are the same all over the world despite their superficial differences.

Okay—there's still work to be done on that paragraph. And there's nothing officially *wrong* with the first version either. It's just that the first version is unvaried and, as time goes on, will prove monotonous. *I* did this. *I* went there. *I* did that. In the second version, we have a short declarative sentence followed by a longer, more complex one, followed again by a short one. The lesson here is not to count every word of every sentence to make sure that if you have fifteen in one, you should have thirty-two in the next. Rather, the idea is for you to *hear* the rhythm of the sentences and mix them up. And, again, the best way to hear sentences is to read them out loud. (I'm not going to keep repeating that Duke Ellington quote, but you get the idea.)

Don't Quote Me on This

A final bit of advice to keep in mind as you make your way through this third-draft stage: do not embellish your piece with quotations. One of my pet peeves is picking up a student essay and seeing a line like this:

As the nineteenth-century Scottish essayist and historian Thomas Carlyle once wrote, "A man without a goal is like a ship without a rudder."

Or one like this:

As the great American humorist Will Rogers, tragically killed in a plane crash, once said, "Being a hero is about the shortest-lived profession there is."

Hey, folks—we're not stupid. We know you went to *Bartlett's Quotations* or some Internet site like BrainyQuote.com, punched in a subject heading like GOAL or HERO, and up came good ol' Tommy Carlyle and Will Rogers. We know that most seventeen- and eighteen-year-olds don't go around spouting Carlyle and Will Rogers—and probably never heard of them before they went shopping around for a quotation. The news flash is that these sorts of quotations don't do anything to make your piece any more important or significant. In fact, they have quite the opposite effect and will only make your essay feel inauthentic and pretentious. Remember—you're not a toastmaster. You're a student writing a personal narrative. Keep it personal.

Although all of these concerns that we've been talking about in Step Eight may seem like a lot to keep track of, the good news is that the more you become aware of these issues, the more you can improve your writing above and beyond the college application essay. Problems like adverb and adjective abuse and vague reference can really pull down the level of your writing, so you may as well see your college application essay as an opportunity to get a grip on these problems and vault ahead. Now, on to the polish.

Recap

1. Less is more. Go easy on the metaphors and stick with the active voice.

2. Avoid exclamation points except for commands or to indicate extreme urgency, as in yelling "Fire!"

3. Substitute strong verbs for adverbial phrases.

4. Reserve dialogue for important moments, not to convey exposition. Keep the dialogue short and try to capture and vary the voices. When in doubt, don't use dialogue, for bad dialogue is far worse than no dialogue.

5. Be conscious of your reader's time and don't waste it.

6. Avoid repetition of words within a sentence and from sentence to sentence.

7. Go easy on the adjectives. Don't rely heavily on a thesaurus.

8. You're less likely to lose your way in a sentence if you place your subject and verb near the beginning.

9. Check your pronouns to make sure you're not falling into the "vague reference" trap.

10. Vary your sentence structure.

11. Don't try to "dress up" your narrative with fancy quotations from famous people.

Pulling It Together

At this point in the essay-writing process, I bet you just want to be done with the thing. Chances are, you're alternating between being pleased with your piece and finding it absolutely without merit. Why can't I be a better writer? Why is my language so flat and clumsy? How will my piece compare to those of my competitors vying for admission to the same schools? These are the kinds of questions that you're badgering yourself with.

Let me say, as clearly as I can, that pestering yourself with such questions at this stage of the game is seriously counterproductive. There's still work to be done, and you have to discipline yourself to do it. One way to start is by finding something to admire about your writing. Enjoy what's there to be enjoyed and energize yourself with positive feelings so you can finish the job. After all, it's absolutely essential to hang on to positive feelings if you're planning to give your piece out for critical readings—the next step in the process.

Reviews: Making the Best of It

By the time you apply to college, you should be fairly experienced at receiving critical feedback. Teachers and peers have reviewed your work over the course of your student career and may have given you very blunt critical input. It's one thing, however, to get a poor review on a paper that explores the causes of the Crimean War or that analyzes Milton's use of allegory in *Paradise Lost*. It's quite another to receive a thumbs-down on a personal narrative in which you've tried to write honestly and affectingly about someone or something you've loved and lost or that time you nearly drowned in the ocean and had to fight your way back to shore. When you put yourself out there in such a naked way, it can really hurt to get a negative review.

In preparing yourself for such a possibility, it helps to know that anyone who has ever written anything has encountered naysayers, no matter how great that writer's ultimate acclaim turned out to be. The *Morning News*, an online magazine, has compiled a selection of one-star reviews culled from Amazon.com. In these reviews, readers heap scorn upon novels that *Time* magazine has ranked among the 100 greatest of the twentieth century. Here is a sampling of put-downs:

Catch-22 by Joseph Heller

"Obviously, a lot of people were smoking a lot of weed in the '60s to think this thing is worth reading."

The Catcher in the Rye by J. D. Salinger

"So many other good books . . . don't waste your time on this one. J. D. Salinger went into hiding because he was so embarrassed."

The Lord of the Rings by J. R. R. Tolkien

"This book is not readable because of the overuse of adverbs."

Now we can wager that these reviews were not necessarily the work of great thinkers, and certainly Joseph Heller, J. D. Salinger, and J. R. R. Tolkien garnered enough in royalties, awards, and *good* reviews to help cushion the blow. But a bad review can give even a secure and accomplished professional writer a sick feeling in the stomach, and, at some point or another, everyone gets a bad review.

Soliciting readings of your essay from a number of different readers is a good thing to do as you near the end of this project because, even if you don't actually do anything with any of the criticism, you still know that you put your work out there and, in doing so, can honestly say you've explored the relationship between the writer, the reader, and the piece of writing. At earlier points in this book, I've talked about getting readings, but I haven't focused on the need to approach feedback with the right attitude and the right questions. So let's look at some guidelines:

1. **Know that all critical feedback is not created equal.** When you receive feedback on your piece, it will be readily apparent whether or not your reader has read your work with attention and openness. Hopefully, you'll be able to sense a responsiveness and engagement coming from the reader, along with some good questions. If you don't feel you're getting a sensitive and engaged reading, then there's no need to take the feedback to heart.

2. **Be open to good feedback from unexpected sources.** You never knew Aunt Dottie could be so sharp, but guess what? She's given a really on-target reading of your work. By the same token, your English teacher, who has some fine qualities, is not necessarily so gifted when it comes to providing useful feedback. You will have to try to be a discerning critic yourself when it comes to receiving criticism.

3. **Listen—don't defend.** Assuming a defensive posture around critical feedback does not serve any useful purpose. Telling yourself that your reader is a jerk or mean or doesn't know what he's talking about may salve a hurt feeling for the moment, but it would be much better to just hear what your reader has to say, assess it as dispassionately as possible, and move on to your next course of action. If your reader has not given you what feels like a thoughtful reading, then you may choose to discount it. But if you suspect that there's something valuable to be had from your reader's critique— even if that critique has hurt you—then you will want to consider it carefully and take what you can get from it.

4. **Be alert to common themes.** Are you finding consistent points emerging from the different critiques? *Too confusing*, some say. *I can't relate to the characters. I didn't get the point of the whole thing.* Your average reader, who may not be particularly skilled in the fine art of giving critical feedback, will probably speak in generalities, such as those above, and may not have anything specifically constructive to say. Then again, it's the work of the critic to point out flaws, not to fix them. Fixing flaws is the job of the writer. You'll want to keep your ear attuned to any common themes you're hearing back from your readers, because if two or three people say the same thing, then you may very well have a problem that needs to be solved.

5. **Tell yourself it can be fixed.** Most things can be. If your reader feels that your piece is too confusing, you may have to alter the structure. If people aren't relating to the characters, you'll have to examine the actions of those characters or their language or the point of view to try to figure out what's

wrong. If The Point of your essay isn't coming across, then you may have to state your point more explicitly . . . or perhaps less explicitly. In fact, it's entirely possible that you have misconstrued The Point of your essay and believe your piece is really about friendship, let's say, when, in fact, it may actually be more of a story about healthy competition. Examine your piece from all different angles to see whether you've missed something, but, whatever you do, don't despair—the essay may only require a little extra investment of energy to get it right.

6. **Realize when enough is enough.** At a certain point, you should be able to tell yourself that what you've written is good and that you don't feel the need for any more input. If you were lucky enough to find a half dozen or so readers— teachers, family members, friends—then that should suffice. You don't want to worry your piece to death, fiddling with it until all the juices have run dry. Let your piece have its readings, and then reel it back in for the final work that has to be done.

Keep in mind too that readers bring all of their own baggage to the reading and you have to be able to filter it out, argue against it, simply ignore it, and, beyond a certain point, hold on to your convictions. I have had a number of situations in which I've coached students who have produced really terrific essays, only to have their parents worry and fret over the finished product. Is it showing Johnny in a good enough light? Is it making Johanna look lazy, ditzy, or angry? And then I have to make my argument—that the college admissions essay is a very appropriate forum for a student to air doubts, frailties, and concerns—as long as the writer also indicates self-awareness and growth.

Let me give you an example. I worked with a student who was brilliant in math but rather diffuse in his personal life. That is to say, he had a tendency to lose stuff. He decided to write an essay in which he recalled losing his calculator. It was an excellent essay because it juxtaposed his confidence in the logical world (the world of math) with his relative insecurity in the temporal world, and it did so with humor and insight and honesty. And who can't relate to losing things, right? But his parents worried that this essay might not reflect well on him. They didn't really understand why anyone would want to admit any kind of weakness in this kind of forum. I was able to convince them, however, that it is not a weakness to admit a weakness. It is confessional writing that most people regard as brave and probing.

I should add that students from the most competitive high schools have told me that their college counselors often discourage them from "admitting weakness" in a personal essay. I tell these students that I think the counselors are as invested in the placement success as parents and students themselves—this is their job, after all—and so may not be willing to be as brave as I encourage my students to be. Fortunately, my theories have been validated by the great success of the students I work with, who, by and large, gain admittance to the schools they wish to attend. These students—and their readers—understand that honest and thoughtful self-assessments will never be held against a college applicant.

Polishing

At this point, after you've digested all the feedback and have made significant adjustments—fixing the structure, strengthening the characterizations, clarifying the point—the rest of your job should be a matter of polishing. There's no better word for it—your goal from here on in is to render the finish of your piece as immaculate and jewel-like as possible. As the cliché goes, every "i" should be dotted and every "t" should be crossed.

Fortunately, you have a word processor to do a lot of that work, but although you will certainly want to run your spell checker and grammar checker to catch mistakes, those functions probably won't catch them all.

So, then, let me alert you to some of the more nettlesome errors that can plague student writers—the ones that often elude spelling and grammar checkers:

- **It's/its.** I see mistakes swirling around these two words all the time, and few spell checkers seem to pick them up. *It's* is a contraction of *it is. (It's nice to see you.) Its* is a possessive—that is, the thing that belongs to *it. (How the leopard lost its spots is an old folk tale.)* Try this: if you can substitute *his* for *its,* then *it's* doesn't work. Get it?
- **Their/there.** In the case of *it's/its,* mistakes arise out of real confusion. In the situation of *their/there,* most people understand the difference between the two, but they still make plenty of mistakes on account of carelessness. Note too that your spelling and grammar checkers probably won't catch these mistakes either. Even though you may know the difference between *there,* a noun meaning "a place, position, or point" or an adverb meaning "in, at, or toward that place," and *their,* a possessive meaning "belonging to them," you won't be able to prove your innocence if you're found guilty of making a mistake. So do yourself a favor—conduct a word search on both words, *their* and *there,* to make sure you've used them correctly in each instance in your essay.

- **Lose/loose.** This is another little demon that trips up a lot of people. You *lose* at poker. You carry *loose* change in your pocket. The verb that sounds like *ooze* is *lose*. The word that has a hissy sound that rhymes with *goose* is *loose*. Hear it . . . see it . . . and try to get it right. *Losing* points on little mistakes like these is aggravating and unnecessary.

- **Affect/effect.** I have witnessed a lot of confusion around these two words, which actually represent four distinct meanings. Starting with *affect*, when the accent is on the final syllable (a-FECT), you have a verb meaning "to have an influence on." *The lack of rainfall will affect the performance of the garden.* A second meaning of *affect*, when the accent is on the first syllable (AFF-ect), is much less frequently encountered. This term, meaning "emotion," is mostly used by psychologists, as in *The patient had very little outward affect.* These two words should not be confused with the commonly used noun *effect*, as in *The effect of the ultraviolet light on the growth of the sunflowers was remarkable.* Less commonly, *effect* is used as a verb meaning "to create," as in *Dr. Martin Luther King was trying to effect change through nonviolence.* In general, however, it will serve you well to remember that *affect* is most often used as a verb while *effect* is most often used as a noun, as in "When you *affect* a situation, your actions have an *effect*."

One other note here: Always choose the word *affect* instead of the word *impact* when you're talking about causing an *effect*. It is quite common these days to hear the word *impact* used as a verb— *President Bush's handling of the Hurricane Katrina crisis negatively impacted his approval ratings.* Some readers are forgiving about a lot of things, but, for some reason, find the use of the word *impact* as a verb highly annoying. You could say, *President Bush's handling of the Hurricane Katrina crisis had a negative impact on his approval ratings.* Otherwise, try *President Bush's handling of the Hurricane Katrina crisis negatively affected his approval ratings.*

- **A lot.** Here is another mistake I see *a lot.* This expression, which means "a great deal or a great amount," is *always* spelled as two words—*a lot.* There is no such word as *alot.* Just to confuse matters, there *is* a word *allot*—which means to "assign or distribute by lot." Here's a point that may help you clarify the issue: just as you would never write "alittle," so should you never write "alot."

- **I/me/myself.** People often trip themselves up on the use of this pronoun, so let me try to quickly clear things up for you. You would say, *I am going to the movies tonight.* If you had a friend with you, you would say, *Beth and I are going to the movies tonight.* (Common usage makes allowances for *Beth and me are going to the movies tonight* or *Me and Beth are going to the movies tonight,* but you should avoid such constructions on your college application essay.) How about *The deed was turned over to my wife and I?* Is that correct? In fact, no. You'll hear it a lot (not *alot)* because some insecure people are trying to sound "proper," but the correct English is *The deed was turned over to my wife and me.* Substituting "myself" for "me" or "I" is another choice people sometimes make, but that's not preferred English either. As a rule of thumb, remove the first object and then try the sentence without it. *The deed was turned over to I.* Does that sound right? Hardly. How about *The deed was turned over to me?*

Yes, that's correct, because you're the object of the action—the action being the turning over of the deed—and *I* is never an object, whereas *me* always is.

- **Who/whom.** Here's another one that's a complete mystery for many people. *Whom* is essentially a dying word. You'll rarely hear it spoken, unless you're sitting in the House of Lords, but it's still used in formal writing. The distinction between *who* and *whom* is basically simple. *Who* is the subject form of the pronoun, as in *Who gave you those flowers? Whom* is the object form, as in *Jen's mother was so surprised when Jen walked in with a bouquet of flowers that she forgot to whom she was talking on the telephone.* Of course, in this day and age, if you were to rewrite that sentence as *Jen's mother was so surprised when Jen walked in with a bouquet of flowers that she forgot who she was talking to on the telephone* it would be considered totally correct and, in fact, considerably less stiff and stuffy. Perhaps the only instance in which you'll still see *whom* used regularly is in the salutation of a business letter that begins *To whom this may concern.* To stop worrying about *whom,* try to rewrite your sentences so that you don't need it—as with the example cited above of Jen's mom forgetting who she was talking to on the phone.
- **Good/well.** This is an important one to get right, because if you slip up here, you're going to sound less than fully educated—not an impression you want to convey on your college application essay. *Good* is an adjective; *well* is an adverb. *He did well on the test* is correct. (Writing *He did good on the test* will not have you doing very well on the test.) *This ice cream tastes good* is also correct, as compared to *This ice cream tastes well.* Of course, because common usage changes

the standards of correctness, people say, *I feel good* and *I feel well* interchangeably without raising any eyebrows.

- **Then/than.** When comparing one thing with another, use *than. Paul is taller than Max.* If you're talking about time, use *then. First, I'll study for my test, and then I'll go down to the gym.*

- **That/which.** *That* introduces what is known as an essential clause—one that describes something that is necessary to the sense of the sentence. For instance: *The fastest train is the one that only makes express stops* or *The kind of movie that she likes best is a good old-fashioned romance.* These clauses beginning with *that* are essential to the sentence—indeed, there is no sentence without them—and are never preceded by a comma. On the other hand, *which* is the word to use when introducing a clause that contains incidental or nonessential information. For example: *He takes only fast trains, which are usually those marked express.* As you can see, the sentence can stand on its own with only the first clause—*He takes only fast trains*—so the second clause is incidental and is only there to give additional information. In such cases, you would insert a comma before *which.* Another example would be, *He takes only fast trains, which are usually marked express, to make sure he gets to work on time.* The nonessential clause, starting with *which*, appears in the middle of the sentence and is set off by two commas. Note too that you can often leave out *that* altogether, in order to make your writing cleaner. It is entirely proper to say *The kind of movie she likes best is a good old-fashioned romance* instead of *The kind of movie that she likes best is a good old-fashioned romance.*

- **Altogether/all together.** As you may have noticed previously, I used the word *altogether*, which means "completely" or "entirely." *They were altogether exhausted by the time they got to the hotel.* The phrase *all together* means "in a group." *The horns sounded wonderful when they played all together in the second movement.*
- **All ready/already.** This is an easy one to clear up, too: *all ready* means "completely ready" *(I am all ready for my close-up)*, while *already* means "previously" *(The relatives have already arrived).*
- **All right/alright.** This one is even easier to clear up: just don't use *alright*. No such word. Cross it off your list.
- **Fewer/less.** Most people don't understand the distinction between these two words. The word *fewer* applies to individual units—*There are fewer courses being offered in the history department this year.* The word *less* refers to mass or bulk. *There is less meaning in my life now* or *There is less bran in white bread than in whole wheat bread.* The expression *fewer in number* is just excess verbiage meaning nothing more than *fewer*, so avoid it.
- **No one.** *No one* is always written as two words. There is no such word as *noone*.
- **Insure/ensure.** You *insure* something valuable: *I have to insure my grandfather's gold watch.* The word *ensure* means "to make certain." *By insuring my grandfather's watch, I am ensuring that I will not suffer financial loss in case of a burglary.* Actually, I find the word *ensure* to be a bit stiff and legalistic, so I would almost always substitute the phrase *make sure* in its place.
- **Continual/continuous.** The word *continual* means "intermittent" or "repeated at intervals." *The continual*

beep from the cell phone indicated that the battery was low.
The word *continuous* means "without interruption" or
"unbroken," as in *The continuous drone of her conversation
was getting on my nerves.*

- **Farther/further.** The word *farther* refers to distance. *They
traveled to farther lands in search of opportunity.* The word
further means "more of something," whether it's time,
degree, or quantity. *Further research is necessary to determine
the validity of this theory.*

- **Principle/principal.** I suspect you know this one, but just
to be on the safe side, let's review. *Principal* can be a noun
or an adjective. As a noun, it means "head" or "chief," as
in the *principal of a high school* or *the principal of a firm.* As
an adjective, it means the "highest" or "main," as in *The
principal reason I'm asking you to do this is because I need you.*
The word *principle* is always a noun, never an adjective,
and it means a "basic truth, law, or assumption." For
instance, *The principles of life, liberty, and the pursuit of
happiness are at the foundation of the American Constitution.*

- **Toward/towards.** This is an easy one: these two words
are actually interchangeable in terms of usage, but in
the United States, the preferred word is *toward*, while
in the United Kingdom *towards* gets the nod.

- **Unique.** This is another word that I often see mistakenly
used, but the problem is easy to clear up. *Unique* means
"having no like or equal." It is absolute. *The Mona Lisa is
a unique work of art.* You wouldn't say, *The Mona Lisa is the
most unique work of art* or *a more unique work of art* or *a less
unique work of art.* You don't apply qualifiers of "more" or
"less" to *unique*—as I say, it is absolute. And, while I'm

on this subject, let me also say that "unique" has become one of the most overused words in the English language. Practically everyone I work with appears to be "unique" in one way or another . . . and, hence, by definition, they are not. "Passion" is another word that deserves a rest. People don't just have interests anymore. They must have "passions."

- **Internet/website/email.** The correct way to spell these words, which have been coined relatively recently, is a matter that often confuses writers, and your dictionaries and spell checkers may not be up to speed in this regard. So allow me to share the most widely accepted conventions. *Internet* should be spelled with a capital "I." *Website* is one word and, when used anywhere but at the beginning of a sentence, is not capitalized. The word *email* is spelled just as I'm showing it—no capital (unless at the beginning of a sentence) and no hyphen.

- **Alternate/alternative.** Here's another small confusion that crops up all over the place, especially when these words are used as adjectives. An *alternate* choice is a substitute or second choice, as in *When he found out that they didn't have lobster, he went with the alternate selection of filet mignon.* An *alternative* choice is usually one of many, as in *There was no lobster left, but there were a number of alternative options on the menu.*

- **Lie/lay.** I've saved the hardest for last. Poll a group of any ten people and you're bound to find that nine—or even ten—of them have no idea how to distinguish between these two words. To *lay* means "to put" or "to place" and requires a direct object to give it meaning. To *lie* means to "recline, rest, or stay" or "to take a position of rest." Therefore, you *lay* a blanket on the grass, but you *lie* down on the blanket. *Lie* does not take an object. The situation is considerably complicated by whatever tense is being used.

It really requires a chart to sort this out.

LIE	FIRST PERSON	THIRD PERSON
Present	I lie in bed.	She lies in bed.
Past	I lay in bed.	She lay in bed.
Perfect form	I have lain in bed.	She has lain in bed.
Participle form	I am lying in bed.	She is lying in bed.

LAY	FIRST PERSON	THIRD PERSON
Present	I lay it down.	She lays it down.
Past	I laid it down.	She laid it down.
Perfect form	I have laid it down.	She has laid it down.
Participle form	I am laying it down.	She is laying it down.

Note the word *lain* as the perfect form of *lie*. You may never have seen this word before and, frankly, it is not a word that I can ever remember using in common speech, but at least now, if and when you see it, you'll know what it is.

Jargon

I'd like to close this chapter by talking about a virus that can negatively affect your essay and quickly alienate your reader. That virus is called jargon. *Jargon* is the specialized or technical language of a particular profession, trade, or group of people. It can often sound excluding, smug, and self-important.

Jargon, as the definition suggests, emerges from a variety of fields. We currently have a high volume of business jargon invading our everyday language, as well as jargon from the legal profession, the sports world, the military, show business, and so on. In an earlier section of the book, we talked about clichés, and jargon can quickly generate clichés, once the general population picks up on it. For example, the business world creates jargon—*bandwidth, low-hanging fruit, value proposition, face time, win-win situation*—and although these expressions may, for a while, have some relevancy in the particular field from which they emanate, they sound unspeakably stale when you start to hear them coming out of the mouths of the clerk at the convenience store, the bus driver, and the weatherman.

Think about those trendy expressions spawned by show business and fashion: *bad hair day, extreme makeover, wardrobe malfunction.* Once the person in the street is using these expressions, it is *so over* (which has itself become a ghastly cliché).

Keep your ears open for those expressions that suddenly seem to be everywhere . . . and don't use them. I'm referring to expressions like *bring to the table, bring to the party, at the end of the day, pushing the envelope, thinking outside the box, playing hardball, hitting one out of the park, déjà vu all over again*, and so on. If they feel familiar, it's because they *are* familiar.

The other way that jargon can infect your prose is by clogging it up, turning writing that should be clean and light into something cluttered and leaden. Much of this effect comes from using words that have the self-important ring that characterizes jargon. Good writers and readers particularly loathe the use of the words *utilize* for *use, necessitate* for *need, conceptualize* for *conceive*, and *dialogue* for *conversation* (and make absolutely sure you never use *dialogue* as a verb). The baggy buzzwords of the nonprofit fund-raising world and the world of the social sciences have coated the common tongue so that we now have an overabundance of lofty, empty expressions like *proactive*, *entity*, and *continuum*.

If, heaven forbid, you find yourself borrowing from legal jargon, then you really run the risk of killing off your essay. There's nothing quite so deadly as legalistic language, so steer clear of anything like *aforesaid* or *prior to* or *terminate*. Always go for the simpler word, so instead of *terminate*, use *end*. Instead of *prior to*, use *before*. Always choose *if* instead of *in the event of*, *about* instead of *regarding*, *start* instead of *commence*, and *buy* instead of *purchase*. And under no circumstances should you ever use the expression *at this point in time* instead of *now* or you might really have your readers tearing out their hair.

After years of working with students, I have developed my own Top Ten list of words I hope never to see again in any admissions essay with which I come into contact. A little drumroll please, and here they are:

- Potential
- Goal(s) (unless we're talking about an actual goal in a sports game)
- Success
- Transformation
- Opportunity
- Empowerment
- Commitment
- Competence
- (The) Future
- Passion

With regard to these, all I can say is *Show me, don't tell me.* I don't want to see a lot of words that make these essays look like they're fund-raisers for a college or hospital. I want to see *you.* In another sphere of my professional life, I work as a marketing communications consultant for colleges and universities (yes, I often write those big, glossy viewbooks that you take home from your college visits, or development materials like annual reports or solicitation letters that go out to prospective donors). In those situations, like it or not, I'm often called upon to use words from the preceding list and that's just the way it is. You, however, do not want to sound like the Voice of an Institution. You want to sound like a human being . . . which you are . . . so please write honestly and in a very real way from your heart.

All the guidelines mentioned in this chapter are simply that—guidelines. This chapter is not intended to serve as the last word on the issue of polishing. Rather, I am simply addressing the most common mistakes I see from student writers. If this helps, then that's great. But perhaps the best advice I can offer on the subject of polishing is to allot (not *a lot*) enough time before the due date so that your panel of readers can look over your piece for polishing and proofreading purposes. In terms of typos alone, it's amazing how a new set of eyes can pick up mistakes that have eluded your own eye over the course of many readings.

Recap

1. Energize yourself with positive feelings to finish off the job.

2. Prepare for critical feedback by following recommended guidelines.

3. Use the spelling checker and grammar checker functions on your word processor, but don't rely on them exclusively. You still have to be responsible for proofreading.

4. Familiarize yourself with common usage errors and avoid them.

5. Steer clear of jargon.

STEP TEN

Finishing Up

As we've discussed, one of the more difficult aspects of being a writer is the fact that you can never make a piece of writing perfect. Some writers come miraculously close, but, as a rule, even they can ultimately find something about their finished product that dissatisfies them. I've published a number of novels, and I must say it's very frustrating to see one's work in print, between hard covers, and know that you could have made it better somehow. One antidote to this kind of frustration is to scrupulously avoid what you've written once you're past the point of being able to do anything about it. But you're not at that point yet—there's still time for you to make your piece even better.

In your situation, as you enter the final stage of this process, your aim is to walk the tightrope between assiduousness and acceptance. On the one hand, you want your piece to be as finished as possible. On the other hand, you have to be able to let go of it when the time comes, and to feel good about letting go. Knowing that you've done your all for the piece is the best way to move toward a positive feeling of acceptance around it rather than a dispirited sense of resignation.

Right now I'd like to remind you that the work of writing is just that—work. Hard work, and lots of it. When you look at a sentence that you know has a problem but can't quite put your finger on what that problem is, the labor involved in the problem solving can be mentally exhausting. Sometimes you'll read a sentence a dozen times over and with each successive reading your brain feels a little more fried. You can endure that experience as long as you know that the problem does not stem from your inadequacy but, rather, that problems are an inherent part of the writing process and fixing problems is what writers do, the way fixing pipes is what plumbers do.

As you get used to writing, you'll find ways to relieve the fatigue that accompanies the work. You'll get up and walk around between the eighth and ninth time you read a problem sentence. You'll make a cup of coffee. You'll do twenty push-ups. And then, somewhat recharged, you'll go back into the arena, and, lo and behold, you'll discover that all you had to do to fix your problem was to simply cut out a couple of words you didn't need, or reverse the order of some words, or deal with some other minor issue that was easy to handle once you diagnosed what was wrong.

I want to spend a few moments giving you a picture of the kind of hard labor I engaged in when I was writing this book. Let's look at the last paragraph of the previous chapter, Step Nine, to see how that evolved:

> All the guidelines mentioned in this chapter are simply that—
> guidelines. This chapter is not intended to be a do-all/be-all
> approach to the issue of polishing. Rather, this is strictly
> a round-up of mistakes that I commonly see from student
> writers and if ~~it~~ this little crash course helps you, then that's
> great. Perhaps the best ~~piece of~~ advice I can give you about

polishing, however, is to allot (<u>not a lot</u>) enough time (~~not a lot~~) before ~~you have to send it in~~ <u>its due date</u> to allow for others to look at it for polishing and proofreading purposes. Even just in terms of typos, it's amazing how a new set of eyes can pick up ~~these~~ mistakes that your eye has ~~gone~~ <u>passed</u> over multiple times.

Most of my self-editing at this stage was done with three goals in mind: to increase clarity, to create prose that was more vivid, and to eliminate any words that would hold up the flow of that prose. So, if you look at that first edit—where I changed *it* in the third sentence to *this little crash course*—you can see that I was not only addressing the issue of vague reference (what exactly was *it* anyway?), but I was also trying to make things a little livelier. Moving along to the second edit, I realized that the parenthetical phrase (not *a lot*) was in the wrong place, so I moved it. I then changed *before you have to send it in* to *before its due date* because I felt that I needed to get rid of some boring words. Similarly, I realized I didn't need the word *for* to follow *allow*, so that was yet another word saved. Again, in the last sentence, I saw that I could do without the word *these* and decided that the word *passed* was livelier than the word *gone*.

So was I done? Not quite. When I sat down to read it again after a day's rest, more changes came to pass:

All the guidelines mentioned in this chapter are simply that— guidelines. This chapter is not intended to ~~be a do-all/be-all approach to~~ <u>serve as the last word on</u> the issue of polishing. Rather, ~~this is strictly a round-up of mistakes that I commonly see from student writers~~ <u>I am simply addressing the most common mistakes I see from student writers</u>. ~~and if~~ <u>If</u> this ~~little crash course~~ helps ~~you~~, then that's great. ~~Perhaps~~ <u>But perhaps</u> the best advice I can ~~give you~~ <u>offer on the subject</u>

of ~~about~~ polishing~~, however,~~ is to allot (not a lot) enough time before ~~its~~ the due date ~~to allow for others to~~ so that your panel of readers can look ~~at it~~ over your piece for polishing and proofreading purposes. ~~Even just in~~ In terms of typos alone, it's amazing how a new set of eyes can pick up mistakes that have eluded your own eye ~~has passed over multiple times~~ over the course of many readings.

Well now, that's something, isn't it? As I moved along in this process, my paragraph was more marked up. It's supposed to be the other way around, isn't it? *Fewer* changes as you go along? Ideally, that would be the case, but what you're really doing when you edit is artfully using your machete to clear away the brush. As the writing that's worth saving emerges, you achieve greater clarity and ever greater impact.

So let's look at my changes. I decided, as I went along, that I didn't like that *do-all/be-all* phrase. It sounded like I was trying too hard to be clever, at the cost of clarity. I decided to go with *the last word*—not the freshest phrase, perhaps, but one that easily and effectively telegraphs its point. The next sentence that I changed—*Rather, this is strictly a round-up of mistakes*—suffered from the nagging problem of vague reference. What exactly did *this* refer to anyway? I rewrote that sentence to be less vague—not to write a gorgeous sentence, but a very clear one.

Issues Not to Worry About

The next interesting change to look at in the revised paragraph is the sentence that begins *But perhaps the best advice I can offer.* Now I bet you're going to tell me that there's something wrong with that. You're not supposed to start a sentence with *but* or *and*, right? To that, I reply, *Don't worry about it.* Too many people worry about rules of writing that are no longer adhered to—like the admonition not to start a sentence with a conjunction. To avoid something so presumably dire as starting a sentence with the word *but*, they'll substitute a word like *however*. The sentence sequence I changed would then read: *If this little crash course helps you, then that's great. However, the best advice I can offer. . . .* Now there's nothing wrong with using the word *however* in that context, but I have to admit I don't love it. It sounds a little stiff and formal, which, coming after the phrase "crash course," makes it feel even less appropriate. So I decided to start the sentence with *but*, knowing that it was totally within my rights to do so. (As to whether or not you can start a sentence with the word "However," indeed you can—just put a comma after it.)

A lot of people shy away from starting a sentence with *and* or *but* because their elementary school teacher told them it was a bad thing to do. In explaining sentence structure, teachers often stress the perils of sentence fragments and might give examples of fragmented sentences like *John and Mary went to the beach. And had a good time.* That, they will tell you, is altogether wrong—and they're right. *And had a good time* is a fragment because it lacks a subject. But in teaching their lesson that way, some instructors wind up convincing their students that you must *never* start a sentence with a conjunction. Not so.

Now look at these sentences:

John and Mary went to the beach. And they had a good time. They certainly were surprised, because they almost never enjoyed the beach, as they were both redheads and burned easily.

Is that second sentence wrong? Not at all. It was my conscious decision to start that sentence with a conjunction. As you read on to the third sentence, you discover that John and Mary usually don't do very well at the beach. They don't much like the sun because, as redheads, they burn easily. So there's a certain kind of irony that's underscored by the sentence structure here. They went to the beach. *And* they had a good time—surprising even themselves. If it had been written as *John and Mary went to the beach and had a good time*, we probably wouldn't have even noticed it. But the break between the two sentences makes us sit up a little and lets us share John and Mary's surprise over the experience. (And there we just had another sentence that starts with *but*.)

Of course, we don't want to begin the majority of our sentences with *and* or *but*. We want to use this technique selectively and with justification, such as in the case above. So think about how you're using this technique, and derive the rules from what makes sense for your piece, not from what your elementary school teacher once told you.

While we're on the subject of issues we needn't worry about, here's another one to cross off your list: split infinitives. An infinitive is the form of the verb that comes after *to*, as in *to celebrate* or *to complain*. A split infinitive occurs when a word is inserted between *to* and the verb, as in *to joyfully celebrate* or *to bitterly complain*. That phantom elementary school teacher from your childhood may still be hectoring you never to split your infinitives, but the *Chicago Manual of Style*, a bible for writers everywhere, claims that it hasn't worried about split infinitives since its thirteenth edition, published in 1983, so why should we?

If you're genuinely concerned that a college admissions counselor might relegate you to the reject pile on account of a split infinitive, you can protect yourself easily enough. All you have to do is be aware of the split infinitive issue, and rewrite accordingly. So if your sentence reads, *Mrs. Lopez stopped her landlord on the staircase to bitterly complain about the lack of heat*, you can rewrite it as *Mrs. Lopez stopped her landlord on the staircase to complain bitterly about the lack of heat.* Personally, it's not the kind of thing I'd worry about. There are far more urgent issues to attend to.

Gender Sensitivity

If you're concerned about elements in your essay that might distract or otherwise trouble a college admissions counselor, one issue that is certainly more pressing than split infinitives is gender sensitivity. Your essay could very well be read by a man or woman who might be negatively impressed by sexist, stereotyped language and thinking. To make sure you're not found guilty of such transgressions, follow these guidelines:

1. **Be alert to the fact that not all people are created men.** In days gone by, it was routine to see two sentences go together like so: *An engineering major at MIT has to be an analytical thinker. He has to be comfortable with logic.* We now acknowledge that MIT engineering majors are often women, and so that second sentence would act as a challenge to a great many readers— perhaps including the college admissions counselor who's reading it. So you'd want to rewrite those two sentences. You have two choices. The first sounds like this: *An engineering major at MIT has to be an analytical thinker. He or she has to be comfortable with logic.* "He or she" is perfectly correct, but sounds a little clunky to some ears, mine included. So what I would do is to rewrite it as follows: *Engineering majors at MIT have to be analytical thinkers. They have to be comfortable with*

logic. By using the gender-neutral plural in this instance, you sidestep any problems.

2. **Watch your gendered nouns.** Outmoded language is one remnant of living in a culture that was once a lot more overtly sexist than it currently is. At one time, a person who fought fires was always referred to as a *fireman*, just as a person who delivered the mail was the *mailman*. As a culture, however, we haven't evolved so completely that we don't have to worry about old, sexist language leaching into our writing. Therefore, you'll have to read your essay carefully to make sure you've found and corrected outmoded words and expressions. Here is a short list of those to look out for:

Old	Current
Fireman	Firefighter
Mailman	Letter carrier
Caveman	Cave dweller
Freshman	First-year student
Chairman	Chairperson
Mankind	Humankind, people
Man the booth	Staff the booth
Man-made	Machine-made

Note too that certain words that were used in the past to denote gender are now considered inappropriate and even silly. Therefore, writers who use nonsexist language will abjure such terms as *steward* or *stewardess*, but will instead use the phrase *flight attendant*. Words such as *authoress* or *poetess* or *sculptress* or *executrix* have been phased out in favor of non-gender-specific words like *author, poet, sculptor*, or *executor*. On the other hand, one would still use the word *midwife* to denote a woman or a man who assists women in childbirth. (Note that I was sensitive not to say *man or woman*—make sure you don't always put the man first in such situations.) The word *midwife* means "with the woman," which describes the action of the job, whether you're a woman or a man. Also, you want to be careful not to tell us the obvious, such as "Ellen Brown is a female architect" or "Sandra Li is a female radiologist." We can figure stuff like that out for ourselves.

3. **Give women the same respect you give men.** If you're writing about Bill and Hillary Clinton, make sure you don't refer to him as "President Clinton" and to her as "Hillary." It's either "Bill" and "Hillary" or "President Clinton" and "Secretary Clinton." If you're writing about Brad Pitt and Angelina Jolie—for some unimaginable reason—don't refer to him as "Pitt" and her as "Angelina." That will feel sexist and disrespectful to many readers.

These points may seem minor to you, but remember that your narrative is going to be read by a real live person who might react negatively to sexist language, so why risk it?

Proofreading

You are now beyond the point where you're going to be worrying about structure, characterization, or even technical issues like word choice. We'll assume all of that has been taken care of already, and right now you're only dealing with the final details. But, as I've said, lack of attention to these final details can hurt your cause, so this is not a time to fall down on the job. I just received a letter the other day from my alma mater, a major university of great prestige that was soliciting contributions for its annual fund, and right there in the second sentence was a typo. I couldn't help but think that if they couldn't get a letter right, how would they put my money to good use? So I didn't make a contribution. (Well, to be perfectly honest, the fact that I had to get a new set of snow tires for my car influenced my decision as well.) In this situation, however—as in most situations you'll encounter in life—neatness counts. If an admissions counselor has to figure out that you wrote "of" when you meant to write "on," it's going to take more of his or her time and you may not gain favor as a result. The counselor might think you're kind of sloppy and might wonder whether you can handle the workload at college. And who needs to have an admissions counselor thinking thoughts like that about you?

As I said in the last chapter, you're going to round up your panel of readers and hope they'll be able to catch mistakes for you. The ultimate responsibility for catching mistakes, however, rests with you, so, for the purposes of the college application essay and everything else you write in the future, here are some good techniques to use as you proofread:

1. **Give your eyes—and brain—a rest.** It helps to proofread when you give your eyes and brain a chance to see your work in a way that is relatively fresh. Sleep on your final draft for a night and look it over the next day. You'll have a better chance of catching mistakes that way.

2. **Print it out.** Some people claim that they can see mistakes on a computer screen just as well as they do on the printed page. I doubt it. I certainly can't, but then again, I'm not of the generation that was born and raised on PCs. At the very least, experiment. Try proofreading on the screen and then on hard copy to see what works best for you. When you

proofread, also try examining one sentence at a time. Use a tape measure or ruler to block out every sentence except the one you're looking at. This forces you to focus.

3. **Play with the graphics.** Your aim is to wake up your eyes—to give them the print equivalent of a double latté with an espresso shot. One way I do that is by increasing the size of the font on my hard copy. If I use a 10-point font on the original, I might blow it up, for proofreading purposes, to a 14-point or even a 16-point font. While you might decry this practice as being wasteful of paper, we're talking about the difference between one and a half printed pages or two and a half printed pages for an essay of this length. And you'll be amazed at how many more mistakes you can catch that way. You can try changing the color of the ink as well, if you think that might help refresh your eyes. Just be sure to return your text to the recommended formatting before you send your final version to the schools you're applying to.

4. **Proofread for one kind of error at a time.** Professional proofreaders can do it all at the same time—spelling, punctuation, and so on—but then professional proofreaders are a breed unto themselves. We lesser mortals will do much better if we isolate our tasks. For instance, begin your proofreading by checking for spelling errors. Any word that doesn't come naturally to you should be given special attention. Keep a dictionary handy. Some people use the trick of reading a paper backward to check for spelling errors. This way they're not swept up in the sense of the narrative, but, rather, are just looking at words that read as if they have no relation to each other and are therefore easier to isolate for the purposes of checking them. After applying yourself to the spelling end of things, you might then want to turn to

something like commas. Circle and examine every comma in your paper to make sure you're using it correctly. We will not be going into the issue of correct comma usage here—that's beyond the purview of this book—but through your English teacher, your school librarian, or the Internet, you'll be able to locate many sources that can bring you up to speed on this issue.

Break Out the Rocky Road

When your work is finished, give yourself a treat—an ice cream sundae, a six-hour nap, a movie marathon, or whatever you choose. You should be able to tell yourself that you've worked with real concentration and focus and have earned your reward. Then you can mail off your application and sit back and wait. Whatever happens, you can honestly say you did your best, which is all that any of us can do.

So then, our work here is almost finished, and I wish you much luck, but there are two more sections of this book that merit your attention: appendix 1 and 2. In appendix 1, you'll see, in step-by-step analyses, how other student writers have handled the assignment of the college application essay with grace, talent, and a lot of hard work. It's a great place to gain a few more good ideas and insights into this demanding process we've been examining. Appendix 2 goes beyond the personal statement to offer some strategies for how to approach the overall essay-writing demands of the college admissions process.

Recap

1. There are some issues you don't have to worry about, no matter who tells you otherwise. You can, for instance, start a sentence with a conjunction, and split infinitives are acceptable as well.

2. Use gender-sensitive language and gender-neutral forms for occupations, such as *firefighter* instead of *fireman*.

3. Proofread carefully.

4. Give your eyes and your mind adequate rest before proofreading.

5. Try proofreading from hard copy to see whether it helps you catch mistakes.

6. Experiment with font size and ink color to see whether that helps you catch mistakes, but always remember to return to the correct formatting before sending in your final version.

7. Try proofreading for one kind of error at a time. For instance, start with spelling and then move on to commas.

APPENDIX 1: REAL STUDENT ESSAYS

All along, I've been emphasizing the idea of writing as process, and now it's time to explore this process further by examining the evolution of a few sample essays. These essays are not featured here because they are works of incomparable splendor—the Sistine Chapels of college application essays. Surely, there have been and will be better essays than these. But, that said, the authors of these essays labored over them with commitment and conscientiousness. All felt good about their product, as they deserved to, and they were all admitted into excellent colleges and universities.

Every one of these writers went through the prescribed process—a series of drafts and a polish. Every one of them had difficulty fixing on a topic, locating the conflict, structuring the narrative, and determining The Point or the *why* of the essay. They all had to overcome significant resistance—that nefarious force that can short-circuit the work of any writer. What all of these writers had in common was that they committed themselves fully to the process, which, as a rule, is the only way that you can get the writing work done.

We're not going to be able to look at every brushstroke that produced every one of these essays. That would be beyond the scope of what we can do here, and it would probably also be quite tedious. What we're going to do instead is look at some of the *highlights* of the editing process, as seen through the development of five sample essays. Let's start with Megan.

Megan

Megan was a very serious, accomplished student at an exclusive private school in New York. She aspired to go to a top private college and needed an essay that would keep her in the running. During high school, she had taken a trip to Cuba and wanted to write something about that. She showed me a rough first draft that was pretty much of a yawn in which she basically talked about her feelings regarding the political system in Cuba. There was very little of Megan in the essay, so we started talking and I offered a few prompts. One of the questions was "What sticks out in your mind as a special moment of that trip?"

After considerable thought, Megan came up with a memory of being in a museum with a Cuban girl who had become a friend of hers. They stood before a painting of some other girls. That's all that Megan said, but, right away, I got the vibrations of a good essay. I like memories like that—ones that come to you strongly but you're not sure why. It usually means that there is plenty to explore, much of it subtle. And there was.

Let's look at an early draft that Megan wrote, based on this memory:

Twenty years ago Cuba was just a tiny island 90 miles south of Miami that had a different system of government and where we were not supposed to travel. I wanted to go to Cuba because I thought it would be an interesting experience, a chance to learn new things, and to witness something firsthand that most people in the United States only know through books and TV. I had no idea that being in this country would change my whole concept of friendship, nor did I think I would forge bonds with people living lives that could not be more different than my own.

Spending the afternoon walking around El Museo Bellas Artes (the fine art museum) with Flora was almost a magical experience. I had barely entered the building when Flora grabbed my arm and was pulling me upstairs. She was so excited to show me all of her favorite paintings. I was excited to learn that we had the same tastes in art since we seem to have a good many other things in common. It is amazing to me how similar Flora and I are considering what different worlds we come from. We both read a lot and love Lewis Carroll. We both think that helping others should be the focus of life. We can even commiserate about the challenges of dealing with frizzy hair. We express ourselves in the same manner. She even shares my pet peeve about peoples' tags sticking out. I got my answer about our tastes in art soon enough. We were wandering through a gallery when I suddenly saw a painting that is perhaps one of the most beautiful pieces I have seen. It depicted a group of girls in shadow. The lightness of the colors that were used and the expressiveness of the strokes so embodied to me the mystery and innocence of childhood that I was immediately mesmerized. No sooner did I walk up to the painting's label and read that its creator's name was Fidelio Ponce than Flora was beside me describing almost verbatim why this was her favorite painting.

Even though I loved walking around the museum with Flora and looking at all the different art, seeing our faces light up at the same pieces of art, knowing that we see the same things in the painters' strokes, my experience distressed me. As I walked through the museum with Flora looking at the artwork, I could not help but feel frustration. I just kept thinking how much Flora would love to see the Metropolitan Museum of Art and how much fun it would be to show it to her. I kept imagining how wonderful it would be to take her through all the galleries, to show her the Cassatts, the Gauguins, and the Degas I love so much. It pained me to think about the fact that no matter how strong our connection might be, in less than a month, I might never see Flora again. I couldn't have ever imagined that someone who lives in such a vastly different environment, who has been "conditioned" to think completely differently than I do about politics and the role of government, can think in exactly the same manner as me on so many other levels. In the logistics of our situations Flora and I may be worlds apart, but in our minds, in our personalities and goals for life, we live so much in parallel.

By going to another country that manifests itself so differently from my own I learned to open myself to new ideas and new ways of thinking, to understand differences and to interact intensely with many people whose experiences and backgrounds were different from my own. But most of all, my time in Cuba taught me about connections with people that transcend artificial barriers, about creating bonds with others that can withstand the test of time.

One of the first things I noticed about this essay is that it was long: six hundred fifty-one words. (At that time, the word limit on the Common App personal statement was only five hundred words.) Now, as I've said, long isn't bad. I'd rather work with a long essay that can be cut down than with a short essay that needs to be built up. However, this essay *felt* long. I was sort of checking my watch as I read it. And I wondered why.

The first thing that came to my mind was—this essay needs more conflict. As Megan and I talked some more, it became clearer to me—and to her—why she was so drawn to the painting. It represented a kind of innocence that was absent from the experience of growing up as a girl in twenty-first-century America. With this in mind, she could go back to the essay and find some new directions.

If you look at that first draft, you'll see a good example of what I meant when I said earlier in the book that you can often lop off a first paragraph without losing anything at all. Another interesting thing to note here is that Megan was a student from a very, very intense and demanding private school in New York City and her writing skills were way above that of the average student . . . but you'd never know it from this first draft. For one example, she was plagued with tense problems from the beginning. So if you're thinking that your own technical issues are embarrassing or discouraging, just remember that most writers don't have an easy time with any of that either, especially not at the beginning.

Here is what a subsequent draft of Megan's essay looked like, with my notes (embedded in bold):

The building is three stories of cinder blocks. Compared to all the colonial buildings around it in Old Havana, El Museo Bellas Artes (the fine arts museum) does not look like anything special. I had no idea what was in store for me as I walked through the doors on that July afternoon, but my friend Flora, who lives in Havana and spends many of her afternoons in the museum, understood the magic that lies inside this dull facade. I had barely entered the building when she grabbed my arm and was pulling me upstairs, so excited to show me all of her favorite paintings. I was excited too to see if we had the same tastes in art since we seem to have a good many other things in common. In fact, I found it amazing how similar Flora and I were, considering what different worlds we came from. We both read a lot and loved Lewis Carroll. We both thought that helping others should be life's focus. We even commiserated about the challenges of dealing with frizzy hair.

I got my answer about our tastes in art soon enough. I loved walking around the museum with Flora and looking at all the different paintings, seeing our faces light up at the same pieces, knowing that we saw the same things in the painters' strokes. I kept thinking how much Flora would love the Metropolitan Museum of Art and how wonderful it would be to take her though the galleries, showing her the paintings by Cassatt, Gauguin, and Degas that I love so much. "Come," she said, pulling me up a flight of stairs. "I want to show you my favorite."

Suddenly we were in front of one of the most beautiful paintings I had ever seen. Three small girls wearing flowing white dresses stood in the shadows, their faces obscured, but the backs of their dresses bathed in light. I could see myself in these girls, consumed by the mysteries of being young and the unknown that lay ahead, contrasted with the freedom, the safe place that you emerge from when you ascend into the world of maturity. **[I think this last sentence needs to be broken up into two thoughts. The last part of the sentence does not come through clearly.—A.G.]** The emotions that this painting evoked in me drew me closer, made me want to find out more about the piece. As I walked up to the painting and read that its creator's name was Fidelio Ponce, Flora was beside me describing why this was her favorite painting. **[Why? I sort of feel like we need to know—in a word or two.—A.G.]**

I had never before had the same connection through art with anyone I knew back in the United States; it is just not something that normally enters into my conversations with my friends. Because we did not have movies or music, school or clothes to talk about, Flora and I both immediately opened up to one another about much more personal things, allowing our connection to be that much deeper. But as wonderful as it made me feel to know that we saw the same things in art, and, even more, in life, my experience with Las Niñas **[What is this? You haven't identified it earlier.—A.G.]** frustrated me. It pained me to think about the fact that no matter how strong our connection might be, in less than a month, I might never see Flora again. I couldn't have ever imagined that someone who lived in such a vastly different environment, who had been "conditioned" to think completely differently than I did about politics and the role of the government, could think in exactly the same manner as me on so many other levels. Logistically, Flora and I may have been worlds apart, but in our minds, in our personalities, and in our goals we lived very parallel existences.

My time in Cuba taught me a great deal about the country itself, but what it really taught me was about myself, and about how to live my life. By going to another country that manifests itself so differently from my own, I learned to open myself up to new ideas and new ways of thinking, to understand differences, and to interact intensely with people whose experiences and backgrounds were different from my own. I was equipped with tools for understanding differences, for learning, and for interacting with others for the rest of my life. Perfect strangers became close confidants, and bonds were formed that will withstand the test of time. But most of all, my time in Cuba taught me that connections between people can transcend artificial barriers and that the strength of a friendship is the most powerful force in the world.

One thing that had happened was that the essay had actually grown in length by this point. It was at seven hundred ninety five words before any of the editing, almost three hundred words beyond where it should have been. But that was all right—Megan was committed. As you can see from the edits, she was still having tense problems, among other issues, but she was engaged in the process. She was looking for the conflict, and this time she was closer to finding it. Obviously, there would be easy places to cut and tighten, as at the end of the first paragraph, when she's already made her point—the shared challenge of frizzy hair—but just keeps going. I also showed her in this draft how to introduce a line of dialogue, a powerful tool that alters the feeling of the narrative and moves it to another place quickly and effectively.

Here's what Megan's next draft looked like:

"Oh, my hair!" I cried.

It had started to shower, and I worried that if I didn't get out of the rain I'd frizz out of control.

"Come on," said Flora, pulling me into a big cinder block building. "I want to show you something in here anyway."

As we entered El Museo Bellas Artes, the fine arts museum of Old Havana, I wondered if Flora and I would have the same taste in art. It was really amazing how much we had in common, considering what different worlds we came from. We both loved to read and had a special affection for Lewis Carroll. We believed that helping others should be life's focus. We could even commiserate about split ends, I thought, as we headed up a flight of stairs. It was hard to imagine that we had only known each other for the two weeks since I first arrived in Cuba on a teen delegation with a grassroots organization called Witness for Peace.

"There it is," Flora said, pointing to the rear wall of a gallery on the second floor.

It was one of the most beautiful paintings I had ever seen. Three young girls in flowing white dresses stood in shadows with their faces obscured, but their backs bathed in light. As I stared at the painting, I could see myself in those girls, poised on the brink of maturity.

"That's my favorite," Flora said. "Las Niñas by Fidelio Ponce."

I had never shared this kind of connection through art with anyone back home. My friends and I talked about movies or music or school or clothes, but, without all that, Flora and I opened up to one another about much more personal things. Somehow we didn't get into any of the petty rivalries that seemed to characterize so much of the interaction in my peer group. It pained me to realize that in spite of our strong connection, when my trip was over in less than a month I might never see Flora again. It was hard to believe that someone from such a vastly different culture, who had been "conditioned" to think in such a dissimilar way about politics and the role of government, could be so much like me on so many levels. Flora and I might have been worlds apart, but in our minds, in our personalities, and in our goals we led parallel existences. Our time together made me realize that connections between people can transcend arbitrary barriers and that friendship can be the most powerful force in the world.

"Time to go," Flora said. As we left, she hooked her arm through mine. Girls in Cuba did that. Even though it felt a little strange at first, it also felt very right, I thought, as we headed outside, where the sun was shining again, as if it had never rained.

Nice job, Megan. As you can see, the essay developed into a real narrative. It feels like a story, and, since we all like to read stories, we feel satisfied on a much deeper, fuller level than we did with those first few versions. The essay does a lot of things we talked about earlier in the book. It starts right in the middle of things. It uses dialogue, but very sparingly, at critical points, to move things along. The physical tracking in the story also moves the narrative along—walking upstairs, walking outside. The conflict in this draft is more tellingly expressed: Megan finds herself in a culture that underscores what she feels is wrong with the culture back home. And the essay tells you quite a bit about Megan: she's involved in an activity that reflects her social conscience, she cares about art, and she's a thinker. And it's all in four hundred eighty words—suitable for the five-hundred-word limit that was in place at that time. Now let's move on to Jack.

Jack

Jack was my son's best friend. He practically lived in my house (when my son wasn't living in *his* house), and so I knew, firsthand, what a great kid he was and how complex he could be. He could also be flaky in a stubborn kind of way—or stubborn in a flaky kind of way, depending on how you looked at it. His parents were getting frantic because Jack simply wasn't getting his college application essay done, so I offered to intervene. He worked up a first draft, clear that he wanted to write something about his trip to Boston to visit his dying grandmother. The story was that his parents wanted him to come with them, but Jack declined because he felt he couldn't get away from his job as a lifeguard. Then he had a change of heart, and he took off after them on his own—a road trip of about three hours during which he got very lost.

Jack thought that the story of his car trip would be enough of an essay, but he was wrong. The early part of our work had to do with tightening the narrative and finding the point. As Jack wrote, he came to see that his piece was about a road trip, but, on a deeper level, it was about exploring the kind of person he is. Let's pick up down the road a piece, as the narrative already began to form:

"Can you tell me how to get to Scituate?"

I wasn't sure where I had made a wrong turn, but I was sure I wasn't supposed to be in Boston. My pride wouldn't let me call my parents for directions, so I pulled into a Dunkin' Donuts and asked the cashier. No help. After driving around for another ten minutes I pulled into a firehouse and asked the firemen standing out front for directions. However, as I heard one of the guys chuckle, "He'll be back," I began to realize I was going to have to call my folks.

"You're where?" my mom exclaimed frantically. I was beginning to get frustrated, so I told her if she wasn't going to help, put someone on the phone that would. My uncle, a native of the Boston area, eventually got me headed in the right direction and I was back on my way. However, when he put my parents back on the phone they made it clear to me that it would be best if I just went home. I felt a little guilty about having my escapades become the focus of the evening for my relatives, but my mind was set and I wasn't turning back now. I had ducked out of work early, and embarked on what had become a five-and-a-half-hour trip. Although I missed dinner, I still wanted to see my grandparents. I hung up the phone and pulled into my uncle's house at nine-thirty with only fumes left in my gas tank.

Walking into the house, I was overcome with a sense of relief and happiness, and as I stood in the living room my grandfather brought my grandmother in on her wheelchair to see me. She was weak and obviously not the same woman that had taught me everything from the Ten Commandments to swing dancing. But as she looked into my eyes her warm smile made me forget her current condition.

At the funeral a few weeks later, my mother reminded me of my trip to Scituate that weekend. As I thought about that trip on the car ride home, I realized that although I can recall many times when my spontaneity has gotten me into trouble, it is because of that quality that I don't find myself asking, "What if?"

I was pleased with the way Jack was progressing with his piece, but there were structural issues. He was conflating two distinct events—walking into the Dunkin' Donuts and querying the firefighters—when he should have used those events to "interrupt" the expository needs of the narrative. In other words, we still needed to know more about what was happening—the actual logistics of that cockeyed trip to Scituate—and we didn't want to wait until the third paragraph to find out. I also felt that Jack needed to intensify the conflict. I happened to know his grandmother and she was a strong-willed, stubborn woman—just as Jack was stubborn. We spoke about this and Jack immediately picked up on the connection. Here's how the essay looked in its final incarnation:

"Can you tell me how to get to Scituate?"

I wasn't sure where I had gone wrong, but I knew I wasn't supposed to be in Boston. My pride wouldn't let me call my parents for directions, so I pulled into a Dunkin' Donuts to ask for help.

"Scituate?" the cashier said. "Can't help you there, man."

Even though all I got at Dunkin' Donuts was a blank stare, I was past the point of no return. My parents had gone to Scituate to visit my grandmother, who was very ill, and I wanted to go too, but I had to work. Later that day, when a thunderstorm closed the beach where I was a lifeguard, I jumped into my car and headed out to join the family. However, after two and a half hours, I was cruising aimlessly through downtown Boston with no sign of finding my way. Even though I was tired of being cooped up in a hot car, my stubborn nature wouldn't allow me to turn back, so I pulled into a firehouse to ask for directions. The firemen pointed out the route, but as I pulled away I heard one of them chuckle, "He'll be back." It was then that I realized I was going to have to call my folks.

"You're where?" my mom cried.

I was beginning to get frustrated, so I told her if she wasn't going to help, she should put someone on the phone that would. My uncle, a native of the Boston area, told me which way to go. However, when he put my parents back on the phone, they said I should just head home. I felt guilty about having my escapades become the focus of the evening, but my mind was set and I wasn't turning back now. I hung up the phone, got back on the road, and, driving on fumes, pulled up to my uncle's at nine-thirty.

Walking into the house, I was overcome with a complete sense of relief and happiness. As I stood in the living room, my grandfather brought my grandmother in to see me. She was sitting in her wheelchair, weak and obviously not the same woman that had taught me everything from the Ten Commandments to swing dancing. But as she looked up into my eyes, her warm smile made me forget her current condition. Instead, I took those few moments to remember how much joy she had brought into my life, and how much her honest, strong, and often stubborn character helped to shape my own.

At my grandmother's funeral, just a few weeks later, my mother reminded me of my trip to Scituate. As I thought about it, I realized that if I hadn't been the spontaneous and somewhat stubborn person I am, I never would have gotten to see my grandmother one last time. My spontaneity and tunnel vision can sometimes get me into trouble, but it is because of these qualities that I seldom find myself asking "What if?"

As you can see, Jack did the necessary work. He strung the events of the story together to create a sturdy framework upon which to hang his reflective inquiries about himself and his character. He recognized his conflict—that he had a stubborn character that could get him into trouble—but the resolution came in viewing that stubbornness, *which he got from his grandmother*, as an integral part of who he is and perhaps the single most important element in enabling him to succeed. It's a simple, likable, engaging narrative that goes beyond the "story" to tell something very real and even profound about the storyteller.

Hannah

Hannah, if you recall, was the student whose sister had suddenly been stricken with a brain tumor. Hannah's essay placed her at a summer drama camp, where she was playing the role of Emily in *Our Town*. Hannah was having an awfully hard time getting her head around this huge episode in her family's life—at least for the purposes of her college essay. When the situation of the rehearsal scene described here came to mind, she was ready to write, and she tossed this off in just a few hours. It needed some polishing, but, other than that, it had come to her all in a piece . . . as writing sometimes does at those white-hot moments when you feel really connected to what you're writing.

"I know you're terrified of this act," said Ann, my director, "but you have to let yourself become vulnerable. We're all here to support you. Trust us. We love you."

We were just days away from performing *Our Town*. I was Emily, I needed a breakthrough, and this was Act Three. At the end of this act, Emily, my character, dies but has the chance to relive a day with her family. She learns that the people around her did not really see what was important in life. Her idealized recollection of human existence is shattered. She is deeply disappointed and saddened by her discovery. The only way to perform this last act is with great emotion. But even though I knew this, I would not allow myself to go to a place where I could really feel Emily's pain and loss.

A few months before I left for this theater program, my sister, Jen, who was living in Chile, suffered a seizure. We learned that it was caused by a brain tumor that had been growing undetected for many years. Jen was flown home immediately for brain surgery. The first time I saw my sister in seven months, she was in the hospital on a stretcher with IVs in her arm. The night before her operation, the doctor told us what could happen during brain surgery. Jen could become paralyzed, lose memory, and she could die. I have never been so sad and terrified in my entire life, and I was so angry that this had happened. As it turned out, Jen came through the surgery well and the tumor was benign, but the horror of the experience stayed with me.

Day after day, we rehearsed the last act and day after day I stayed dry-eyed and emotionless. Talking to Ann, I came to realize why I couldn't get to the feelings that this act required. The scene hit too close to home for me. Death had come so close and I did not want to relive those feelings.

I stood there and said my lines. I tried as hard as I could to not just talk about death, but to allow myself to feel. I couldn't. Ann stopped the rehearsal. She asked a staff member, Howie, to go on stage. "Hold Hannah. Don't let her fall," Ann said, "but try to make her feel physically off balance." Howie held on to my shoulders and pulled me in all different directions. As this happened, I said my lines and suddenly started to cry my heart out. This was my breakthrough.

My sister's illness had thrown me off balance and changed my life forever. When, once again, I was thrown off balance, Act Three changed forever. In that moment, during rehearsal, my defenses fell and I was able to reconnect to the sadness I had felt. I discovered I could go there again safely and grow from this experience. From that moment on, each rehearsal and each performance was done with great emotion. We were days away from performing *Our Town.* was Emily, I had a breakthrough, and that was my Act Three.

And there you have it: roughly five hundred words of choice college application prose. (This one was also written back in the day when the word limit was only five hundred words.) To my mind, this piece does it all. It offers conflict in the extreme—the prospect of death that has touched a happy family and the emotional damage it has inflicted on the storyteller. It has a resounding *why*—the "why" of human existence, which, as Hannah understands it, is about soldiering through and dealing with what you are dealt. It covers "The Once" very deftly, putting us on that stage, but also interweaving the backstory of Jen's illness. And, of course, it is based on The Extraordinary vs. The Ordinary—that breakthrough moment that allows Hannah to throw off the mantle of emotional numbness. It even does one more valuable thing—it shows Hannah hard at work at her craft. In fact, her work in theater was an important part of her college application profile, and the fact that her essay shows her involved in the actual work of acting is a lot more significant than just saying that she played Grizabella in *Cats* or Ado Annie in *Oklahoma!* in high school productions.

Eve

Eve is another student I mentioned earlier in the book. She too is a good friend of my son, and she's the one who had a rocky road in high school. She went to Italy right after graduation, and when she returned and was ready to apply to college, she felt she needed an essay that would somehow address her educational shortcomings. Here is an early draft:

"Let's go out to dinner and we can talk about this," my Dad told me the night he arrived in Florence to visit me. It was Christmas Day, and I had been in Europe for three months and Florence only a week. I was under the impression that I was staying until April 3rd, which would make the trip six months long. So when my Dad mentioned I'd be going home early I thought he meant a few weeks early, maybe a month. I didn't know I'd be flying home in two and a half weeks.

During my senior year of high school I knew I wasn't quite ready for college. I went on the school trip to France my junior year, and visited my brother in Ireland also during junior year. I was born with wanderlust and knew I was ready to venture out of America, for more than a week this time. My friend and I looked up programs we could do, and decided to study Italian in Taormina, Sicily, for six months. This was a big deal for my family, as we do not have the money to do things like this. But my parents know me and understood that it was something I had to do for myself. I did not want them to waste their money on a college experience that I was not ready to have. Come August and September all of our friends went off to their schools while we stayed home and I worked at the Gap and she babysat until we left, October 3rd.

Our school in Sicily didn't begin until the end of October, so instead of flying straight there, we made up an itinerary and traveled our way down. We flew into Ireland, and then went to France, Spain, and the mainland of Italy. When we finally got to our apartment in the school we'd be attending, we were emotionally and physically exhausted. For the month of November there we took beginners Italian courses. While we were there we met so many people who had been to amazing places. We started to create a wish list of our own. We missed hostels, meeting new people every day, and being on the road. We found a bigger, cheaper school in Florence that we wanted to attend after Christmas. We wrote our parents all of this and that we wanted to travel more. The school and apartment being incredibly expensive, our parents encouraged us. Who knew when and if we would ever have that chance again?

We ended up traveling all over Sicily for a few weeks. During the month of December we got to Rome, Pisa, Sienna, Vienna, Prague, and a few places in Germany. It was out of Germany that my friend flew home for Christmas, and I had to get to Florence and find the hotel at which I was going to meet my Dad. It was the most liberated I had ever felt when I finally did find it.

So, I was preparing to go to school in Florence until April. Going home was the last thing on my mind, and it was a little shocking to hear that the money I had in my bank account for this trip was so low that I'd be going home in two weeks. I was upset, because for some reason it was very strange to think of home, when I thought that I had another adventure on the way for my last three months. For the next ten days while my Dad was with me, I caught myself telling him stories about what had happened on my travels, teaching him words so that he could get by in Italian, telling him about the friends I'd made. I realized that back in September I had planned go to Italy to study and live for six months. That didn't happen. Instead, I saw seven countries in three months, and got the experience of my lifetime. I learned that things don't always go as planned, sometimes for worse, sometimes for better. In my wildest dreams, I never would have imagined that I could have done what I did. Now it is over and I am home, working again. My friend just left to go back to study in Florence, and I wish immensely that I was with her, but I have learned to see money in more realistic ways and I know that I can't. Instead, I am getting ready for the next experience in my life, which will hopefully be college. Sometimes you can benefit from venturing out of the norm, because as opposed to before, I cannot wait to go to college. I have learned so much from traveling and it has shown me a side of myself that otherwise I would never have known, and built a character in me that I am so proud of. If I could go back in time, I wouldn't have changed one day out of those three and a half months.

At eight hundred thirty seven words, this was obviously way too long, but that wasn't its real problem. As I've said, better to write long than short. The real problem was that this essay had very little idea of where it was going or where it had been. It was rambling all over the place. The conflict also felt quite unformed. It felt like the conflict had more to do with what Eve didn't get— the opportunity to travel more—than anything else. And at the end she "wouldn't have changed one day" anyway, so where *was* the conflict exactly? Other aspects of the narrative—The Once, The Ordinary vs. The Extraordinary—also needed work. Where was this narrative actually located in terms of time? Why did we need to know that she had been in Ireland or that her friend flew out of Germany? Eve needed to roll up her sleeves and whip this baby into shape. Here's how her next draft looked:

"With the way your finances are looking, you're going to have to fly home in about two weeks," my dad said at dinner, the night he arrived in Florence to visit me for a week.

"What do you mean?" I said.

"You've run out of money, honey. That's just the way it is."

I had been in Europe for three months, and in Florence for only a few days. This was supposed to be a celebration—it was Christmas Day in one of the world's most beautiful cities—but before our food had even arrived, my father was putting an end to any kind of celebration. I had been planning to study Italian for three more months and then return home in April, but now I was being told that I only had money for two more weeks. I was upset, angry, and extremely disappointed. My parents had wanted this opportunity for me, so why were they cutting it short?

That night, I hardly slept, but the next day, as we went through the Uffizi Museum looking at the Botticelli paintings, my mood started to change. I don't know—maybe it was the curative effect of being surrounded by all that beauty—but I found myself realizing how great it was to be sharing this experience with my father. I realized that I had been unfair with him. After all, it wasn't his fault that I had to go home early; it was my own. Just like in high school, I had veered off-track, and, as a result, I had to deal with the consequences. If only I had lived more frugally and paid more attention to my money, I could have bought myself more time. Now I would have to go home, and I wasn't sure what going home would mean. After all, I had come to Italy to get away from all the decisions I had to make about college and my future, and now those decisions would be staring me in the eye again.

Six days later, it was time to say goodbye to my dad. As we waited at the airport, he told me what a great time he had and that he was proud of me. "You took yourself off on a big adventure, Eve," he said, "and that's just what you should be doing at this time in your life." His words meant a lot to me. It had been a big adventure. I had gotten to see a lot of countries and many great sights. Even though my time was being cut short, the fact was that traveling had changed me and opened my eyes. It taught me that there was more to the world than my small town in New York, where I had always felt a little too "different."

Two weeks later, I was back at the airport, waiting for my own plane with a heavy heart but a clear head. I thought about the mistakes I had made, but I realized that I could learn from them. Somehow the future—the thing that had scared me enough to make me leave home in the first place—didn't seem as scary anymore. In fact, I felt ready for it, ready for change. This time, I felt I could get it right.

As you can see, the conflict has begun to come together here. There is conflict between Eve and her father, whom she views as being unreasonable, but then, when that's resolved, the conflict becomes more internal in nature. It really becomes an issue of the gulf between the Eve of the past and the Eve of the future. And it becomes a much more readable narrative, although still some fifty words too long. Note too the more effective quality of the in medias res opening in the second draft, as compared with the one in the first draft. In the first draft, Eve opened up with dialogue that plunged the reader into the story, but the dialogue was boring. Here the dialogue jumps right into the problem, so it arrests our attention.

Here's what Eve's final essay looked like:

"With the way your finances are looking, you're going to have to fly home in about two weeks," my dad said at dinner, the night he arrived in Florence to visit me.

"What do you mean?" I demanded.

"You've run out of money, Eve. That's just the way it is."

I had been in Europe for three months, and in Florence for only a few days. This was supposed to be a celebration—Christmas Day in one of the world's most beautiful cities—but my father was putting an end to any kind of celebration. I had been planning to study Italian for three more months and then return home, but now I was being told that I only had enough money for two more weeks. I was upset, angry, and extremely disappointed. My parents had wanted this opportunity for me, so why were they cutting it short?

That night, I hardly slept, but the next day, as we walked through the Uffizi Museum looking at the Botticelli paintings, my mood started to shift. Maybe it was the immensely beautiful artwork or maybe it was just taking another look at the situation, but, either way, it was incredible to be sharing this experience with my father. I had been unfair with him. After all, it wasn't his fault I had to go home early; it was my own. Just like in high school, I had veered off-track and now I would have to deal with the consequences. If only I had paid more attention to my money, I could have bought myself more time. I had come to Italy to escape the decisions that I had to make about college and my future, and soon those decisions would be staring me in the eye again.

Six days later, my dad and I were at the airport, waiting for his return flight.

"You know, Eve, I'm really proud of you," he said.

"Proud? But I screwed up."

"No, you didn't. You went on a big adventure and that took courage," he said. "That's just what you should be doing at this time in your life."

His words meant a lot to me. It had been a big adventure. I had gotten to see seven countries and, even though my time was being cut short, the traveling had changed me and broadened my views. I saw that there was more to the world than my small town in upstate New York, where I had always felt a little too "different."

Two weeks later, I was back at the airport, waiting for my own plane with a heavy heart but a clear head. I thought about the mistakes I had made, but realized I could learn from them. Somehow the future—the thing that had scared me enough to make me leave home in the first place—didn't seem as scary anymore. In fact, I felt ready for it. This time, I felt I could get it right.

This draft was virtually the same as the second draft, but with fifty-five words taken out—invisibly. It was just a matter of tightening up the writing. Eve came away with a good essay that held the reader's attention and also did some explaining of her situation, but in an intelligent way.

Matt

For our next essay, let's look at a story about a dead pet that's not just a dead pet story. While Matt's first draft focused centrally on the death of his pet, by the end of the process, that event had been placed in the context of something larger. Here's the first draft:

There she was, lying on the veterinary table. I could see the pain and sadness in her eyes and I could feel it; she wasn't ready to die. Two days before, I had accidentally run her over as I was leaving my house with a friend. Although the event took place on the Fourth of July, I still remember it like it was yesterday. I remember the thumping sounds as the car rolled over her body. I remember the look of shock she gave me. Yeah, dogs can't talk, but she really spoke to me with those eyes, and I knew for sure that she couldn't believe her boy, her master, had run her over.

Maggie was an amazing dog. She could jump higher than any other dog I'd ever seen. She could run faster than cars going forty miles an hour and could swim like a seal. But the greatest thing about her was that she was a genuinely sweet dog, and she was my dog. When she died, I felt like a piece of me was lost. She was my best friend, as funny as it sounds. It was, and still is, so unreal to me that I killed her. I mean, the worst possible scenario that could have happened did. It would have been better if she had died the moment I hit her, but she didn't. She stuck around for two agonizing days. At first, everyone thought she was going to be all right, but it turned out she had spinal trauma from rolling under the car and as her spine swelled she became more and more helpless.

Anyway, the day she died I had to go off to a college soccer camp at Wesleyan University in Middletown, Connecticut. This was like a test from God for me to see if I could overcome this horrible situation and focus on the game that I loved. I had conflicting feelings about soccer in the past, but the day I had to go to camp I saw as a fork in the road of my mind. I could either go to this camp and try to play or I could drop soccer for good and let this tragedy get the best of me. I went to the camp at Wesleyan and managed to do all right. I think if I hadn't gone to that camp I would have ended up suffering from serious depression, but playing soccer and being away from home for that week managed to pretty much keep my mind off of what had taken place back home only a couple of days before.

I'm not saying that the experience at soccer camp completely healed me, because I am definitely not completely healed, but if I had taken the other road I don't know what I would have done. Well, it's three months later and I still think about her almost every day, but I definitely feel like it's getting better. I feel like everything in life happens for a reason and as horrible and unbearable as Maggie's death was, there's got to be a reason behind it.

My feeling about this first draft was that it was strongest in the beginning—that first paragraph. As it went along, it began to feel more like a diary entry, and the writing became too offhand. "I mean," "You know"—that sort of thing. I could understand why Matt lapsed into that tone, because the writing of the piece was another way of processing the event. But, having put the feelings out there, he next needed to make it a piece that someone else could satisfactorily experience, not just a piece for himself.

The way he was able to do this was by strengthening the narrative action. He also had to figure out what the story was really going to be *about*. It shouldn't have been left where it was just a story about a dead dog, because how far can another person go with that? After some conversation, we decided that what the story was really about was Matt's resiliency. He'd had a very tough year with soccer, and then came the trauma of Maggie's death, but in fact the two dovetailed in a highly dramatic way. Here's what the narrative read like in its final version:

"That's some write-up you got," my mom said, from the front seat. "Looks like the coach thought a lot of you."

"I guess," I said, leaning back to try to get some sleep during the drive home from soccer camp.

This had been a really bad year for me and soccer. The coach I had been playing with for my whole life was having personal problems and, for some reason, was taking it out on me. I couldn't understand why. I've always loved the game and gave it my all. To me, it's a thinking person's sport, full of passing and teamwork, and when you play it right, it's like art. But this year I stopped loving it.

"Are you okay back there?" my dad asked.

"Yeah. I'm fine."

My parents were worried about me. During the whole soccer mess, they urged me to stay with it and pressed the idea of the soccer camp. They said I had invested so much in this, and if I gave it up now, my college choices could be limited. Sometimes it felt like everything I was expected to do these days was to help me get into college, and I was tired of it.

"We're making good time," my dad said. "We should be home soon."

What was the hurry? I was in no rush to get home. Five days before, as the capper on this nightmare soccer year, I had gone to the vet's with my parents on the morning I was leaving for camp to put my dog Maggie to sleep. A few days before, I accidentally ran her over, unaware that she was following me out of the driveway. She held on for a few days, looking like she might pull through, but by the third day, she couldn't move her hind legs. A spinal cord injury had kicked in and there was nothing that could be done for her. When I held her in my arms at the vet's, I thought of how we had found her running on the road two years earlier—this little stray black pit bull with the lopsided gait—and I couldn't believe she was leaving us. I always thought of her as a real survivor, but her luck had run out.

"Here we are," my mom said, as we turned onto our road.

We live in real country, surrounded by trees instead of people, and it can get a little lonely. Maggie really was one of my best friends, always keeping me company. The morning we put her down was one of the worst moments of my life, and going off to soccer camp was about the last thing in the world I wanted to do. But I did it anyway.

"You okay?" my dad asked, turning around at the top of the driveway to look at me.

"Yeah. I'm okay," I said, and I suppose I was. The year was as hard as anything I'd ever been through, and I had dreaded coming home, but I guess, in the end, I'm a survivor too.

As you can see, the emphasis of the narrative shifted substantially from the first draft to the last—from being about the death of a dog to being about resiliency. The problematic soccer situation takes first position, and the death of the dog is counterpoised against that, as opposed to the way it was in the first version. This way, there's more chance for resolution. We know *why* this story is being told—because it is a reflection by the storyteller on the means by which he was able to survive a very traumatic incident within a very traumatic year. It's an absorbing read and a good presentation of the storyteller's personal qualities. Note too that a pivotal sentence in this essay starts with a conjunction:

The morning we put her down was one of the worst moments of my life, and going off to soccer camp was about the last thing in the world I wanted to do. *But I did it anyway.*

That's a good example of how breaking the rules can sometimes pay off in far more powerful writing. The important thing is to *know* the rules so that you can break them intelligently.

Victor

This last essay is one of my favorites and is interesting to look at for a number of reasons. The writer was a first-generation Chinese American student, living in Iowa. Brilliant at math and science, he had respect as well for the craft of writing.

Somewhere during our discovery process, in which he answered the questions that appear on pages 33 and 34 of this book, the germ of his story emerged. He told me about being with his grandfather in Taiwan and eating ice cream in the back room of some remote, dusty barbershop. The more we probed that story together, the more interesting it became. This is what his early draft looked like:

Against a mosaic of cars, scooters, and jaywalkers was an old guy clad in cheap rubber slippers on a motorcycle, his grandson clutched between his chest and the dashboard. How he managed to see the speedometer, I don't know. Grandpa didn't care how fast he was going, for he never had much concern for the rules. He had strong moral convictions, to be sure, but he never aspired to become the next one in a long line of lawyers and doctors as his parents had wished—instead, he became a risk taker, an entrepreneur.

The summer I was in Taiwan for the first time, the temperature was in the 90s, and the humidity was at 85 percent. The afternoon sun was glaring, what I thought to be "high" noon.

"Your hair is too long," Grandpa had said. He pointed to my shaggy bangs and untamed sideburns.

"No," I denied, an eight-year-old child opposed to any sort of shearing.

"Too long for this weather," he told my mom. "I'm taking him out to cut his hair."

Reluctantly, I had gone with him. We drove to the countryside, and the first thing I saw was not the assortment of blades for razing young boys' hair, but a group of old geezers. Grandpa stood, chatting with them, until a man with a mole on his nose, and a curly hair growing out of it, motioned us in. Under the counter was a case. The man with the mole took up a metal scoop, and out of the case came three wallops of ice cream—one vanilla, one mango, and one pale purple (Grandpa didn't know what that was, either). For an hour, I stood among them—a scene more incongruous than Grandpa's rushing through traffic—four old men and a child licking ice cream cones and playing Chinese chess.

According to traditional Chinese medicine, of which my mom was a firm adherent, anything "cool" was bad for the health, especially for a severe asthmatic like me. That included, but was not limited to, drinking ice-cold glasses of Coca-Cola, licking popsicles, and catching snowflakes on my tongue. Therefore, I spent the first ten years of my life in a mom-induced deprivation of childhood necessities. There's probably no *real* proof that eating ice cream kills you (except for maybe Irv Robbins of Baskin-Robbins fame, who, his son says, got diabetes after his zillionth ice cream cone).

It was almost sundown before we returned home. Mom would never have known if not for the unshortened hair, gooey cheek, and big grin. She and my grandma chastised us for the "health dangers" to which I had just been exposed, but Grandpa just looked at me and chortled.

It was never to happen again. Just a year later, the same afternoon sun would give Grandpa a stroke, debilitating the left side of his body. He is a shell of his former self, but he remains undaunted: defiant of death when the doctor said he had no chance of surviving, unafraid of haggling with a conceited street vendor twice his size, unashamed of exhibiting his pastels of nude women. He still has his driver's license.

Now there were some nice things in the above, but nothing was really hanging together. So we started to zero in. The piece about Victor's mom being an adherent of traditional Chinese medicine and suspicious of things cold was interesting—but seemed to be in the wrong place. Did we need that ending about Grandpa? Sad, but did it serve the story any? What really *was* the story?

As we moved along in the process, we became aware that the story was very similar to stories I've seen from my Asian American students. These are stories of immigration, which, regardless of the ethnicity, are typically about the pull between an old culture, represented by the parents, and a new culture. That tension coming from the mother in Victor's story was the conflict that spurred the action, and by the time we ended the process, the story looked like this:

"Hold on tight!" shouted my grandfather.

As he zoomed through the mobbed streets of Taiwan on his motorcycle, weaving in and out of cars, scooters, and jaywalkers, I sat clutched between him and the dashboard. How he managed to see the speedometer, I didn't know. He was a small man in cheap rubber slippers, risking the life of an eight-year-old boy. And I loved it.

This was my first visit to Taiwan and the first time I had seen Grandpa since I was a year old. My mother and I had been there for three weeks. She and my father had immigrated to the United States before I was born, and although they had assimilated elements of the "American way" into their lives, placing green bean casserole and hash browns alongside fried rice, in many ways they were still ardently Chinese. Details and patience. Obedience. Filial piety.

There had been little fun on the trip so far. Here in Taiwan in the middle of June, the temperature was in the 90s, with humidity creeping upward of 85 percent. I yearned for relief from the weather— an ice-cold glass of Coke or a popsicle, perhaps—but according to traditional Chinese medicine, of which my mom was a staunch adherent, anything "cool" was bad for the health, especially for a severe asthmatic like me. As a result, I sat sweltering in the heat, watching stale Chinese movies on TV and refusing mugs of hot tea, until my grandfather hatched a plan.

"His hair is too long," Grandpa said to my mom, running his fingers through my shaggy bangs and untamed sideburns. "Too long for this weather. I will take him to the barber."

"No," I whined, deeply opposed to any sort of shearing.

"Go ahead," my mom said. "Go with your grandfather."

Reluctantly, I did as I was told. Soon I was perched on my grandfather's motorcycle, giggling with excitement each time he accelerated through a turn, but at the same time dreading the haircut that was to come. If I had to have a haircut, I wanted to wait until we returned to the States, when I could visit my familiar Great Clips.

We drove a good distance into the countryside. Grandpa skidded to a stop in front of a small shop, dismounted, and lifted me off.

As we walked in, what I saw was not the comforting fluorescent lighting and glossy posters of perfectly groomed models that I was used to back home, but a dim space that featured all sorts of oddly shaped instruments and a cluster of old geezers. Grandpa stood, chatting with them for a few minutes, until a man with a mole on his nose, and a curly hair growing out of it, motioned us into a small room.

There was no haircut. Instead, the man with the mole withdrew a carton from a small icebox. I watched as he took up a metal scoop and dished out three dollops of ice cream—one vanilla, one mango, and one pale purple. My mom's rules binding me from afar, I resisted the icy treat for an instant, but then I put her words away. In this strange, almost magical place, my restraints receded, and suddenly I was not afraid of anything. As I licked the dripping, frigid delight, I watched the elderly men play Chinese chess, arguing over strategy and debating moves.

Looking back now, almost a decade later, I find that I have become more and more like my grandfather, who never had much concern for rules. He had strong moral convictions, to be sure, but never aspired to become the next in a long line of lawyers and doctors as his parents had wished. Instead, he majored in English and became a risk taker, an entrepreneur who owned a business exporting orchids. I can't say for sure where I'm going yet, but I know that afternoon I was liberated—free to dream and fly on my own. Since then, I have eaten ice cream whenever and wherever I can.

So why do I love this essay so much? Because it's a small slice-of-life piece that affixes itself to the brain of the reader. When students come to me after having read my book and bemoan the lack of "conflict" in their lives, I tell them not to capitalize that word. Conflict can be small and focused and can make more of an impression than CONFLICT. In this story, Victor portrays a relationship with a grandfather he barely knew who wound up shaping his life. He ushers us to a distant location and opens up a corner of the world. He takes a familiar situation—the intergenerational conflict within immigrant families—and brings freshness to it. These are some of the reasons why I love this piece—and why, I assume, Harvard loved it too, since that is where Victor wound up.

As I said at the beginning of this appendix, these essays may not be the greatest college application essays ever written. The writers were not necessarily the most accomplished students who ever lived. They were bright, hardworking, and, in many ways, quite typical students who committed themselves to the process. I hope that you too will commit yourself to this process, and I hope this book will help you come to a better understanding of the narrative.

APPENDIX 2: CONQUERING THE SUPPLEMENTALS

When I first published *Conquering the College Admissions Essay in 10 Steps* almost a decade ago, I did not have nearly as much experience coaching students as I do now. To be honest, I did not fully grasp the scope of their essay-writing obligations. Now that I know more, I have vast admiration for these supremely busy young women and men, who somehow find a way to handle all the writing that is necessary to complete their applications. They are able to manage their load because they understand the big picture that is demanded by the college admissions process and they apply a suitable strategy for getting through it all. Like them, you too will want to apply a strategic approach to your essay writing so that you aren't overwhelmed either.

Throughout this book, we have focused on the required essay, also referred to as the personal statement, on the Common Application. The Common App, as it is informally known, is a standardized application used by more than four hundred colleges and universities in the United States and various other countries. Until fairly recently, the Common App essay had a limit of five hundred words. In 2013, the limit was increased to six hundred fifty words, and, of course, this could change again in future years. Most of my students make use of that six-hundred-fifty-word allotment, but that is not to say that you will get marks against you if you write somewhat less. (Beware of going too skimpy, however).

At the time of this writing, the Common App offered five prompts:

1. Some students have a background, identity, interest, or talent that is so meaningful they believe their application would be incomplete without it. If this sounds like you, then please share your story.

2. The lessons we take from failure can be fundamental to later success. Recount an incident or time when you experienced failure. How did it affect you, and what did you learn from the experience?

3. Reflect on a time when you challenged a belief or idea. What prompted you to act? Would you make the same decision again?

4. Describe a problem you've solved or a problem you'd like to solve. It can be an intellectual challenge, a research query, an ethical dilemma—anything that is of personal importance, no matter the scale. Explain its significance to you and what steps you took or could be taken to identify a solution.

5. Discuss an accomplishment or event, formal or informal, that marked your transition from childhood to adulthood within your culture, community, or family.

Like the word limit, the essay prompts may also change from year to year. Even so, they will almost certainly ask you to share moments of significance in your life—and, as such, the narrative approach laid out in this book will still apply.

When I work with a student, we always begin with the Common App personal statement, as both students and their anxious parents are eager to square that away early in the summer. The supplemental essays are generally not released until midway through the summer, and, if time permits, students can get started on those as well before the start of senior year. I usually tell students to plan on about three weeks, start to finish, to complete the personal statement. It can take less time and it can take more time, but three weeks is a reasonably accurate time frame for getting this work done.

The attention you devote to the personal statement will also pay off benefits when you come to your supplementals. By then, the lessons you have learned with regard to using a narrative approach will help you enliven those essays about your most important extracurricular activity, how you will contribute to a diverse college community, and even your academic goals and objectives essay. There is no reason, after all, why any essay should ever be flavorless and dull.

Why the Supplementals?

Some top schools, such as Middlebury, Grinnell, and Washington University, do not currently require supplemental essays, but that situation could easily change. In any event, the vast majority of selective colleges do require at least some supplemental essays. How important are these essays? Very.

In an October 31, 2015, interview in the *Boston Globe*, Richard Nesbitt, director of admissions at Williams College, was asked what Williams was looking for in terms of the supplementals. "Who is this student? What are their values? What's important to them? What makes them tick?" replied Nesbitt.

Do the supplementals and the Common App personal statement carry equal weight? Probably not. The personal statement, after all, is the thing that gets you "into the room," and it has to be completely compelling, distinctive, and authentic. The supplementals, on the other hand, should be thought of as significant enhancers (or detractors) from your overall application. In that same *Boston Globe* article, Williams admissions director Nesbitt says that he prefers calling the supplemental essays "personal statements," because they should not be written in the same style as you would write an essay for one of your high school courses. "These need to be in a student's own voice, in a conversational tone," said Nesbitt. "These are not something we grade; it's more about completing the picture of who this student is."

That idea of "completing the picture" is central to your work on the supplementals. The purpose of these essays is to allow the admissions committee to gain more knowledge about you so that they can make the all-important decision as to whether you should help populate their incoming class. You can be sure of one thing: the admissions counselors will definitely compare your supplemental essays to your Common App personal statement. They will be looking to see that there is a consistency of tone and effort.

Consistency of tone is very important because you don't want it to appear that you had professional help with your Common App essay—even if you did. That is to say, one essay can't be first-rate and the others third-rate because such a discrepancy will be red flags. By the same token, consistency of effort—or the lack of it—will also be readily apparent. If you have left your supplementals to the last minute and they are half-baked, then you will be announcing to the world that you do not plan your time well, and this will give the admissions committee significant pause.

One reason why the admissions process in the United States has become so demanding is because the numbers at the top schools are so daunting. A school like Yale, let's say, gets more than 30,000 applicants for fewer than 1,500 places—an acceptance rate of somewhere around 6 percent. The rigor of the difficult application is just one way to separate the chaff from the wheat, if you'll excuse that rather heartless expression. Let it also be noted that some schools like Yale, Harvard, and Duke have so-called "optional" essays. In other words, these are essays that are labeled optional but, in fact, that word must be taken with a grain of salt if you're applying to a school with a 6 percent acceptance rate. Otherwise put, virtually none of my student writers forego those optional essays.

I'd like to offer one more thought while we're on the subject of "Why the Supplementals?" On January 20, 2016, the Harvard Graduate School of Education released a major report entitled *Turning the Tide: Inspiring Concern for Others and the Common Good Through College Admissions.* Expected to be widely influential, the report calls upon colleges and universities to render the admissions process more humane, less focused on off-the-charts accomplishments, and less geared toward affluent students who have the resources to pursue such privileges as independent research and plum internships.

Because of this move, the emphasis on essays will be greater than ever. Frank Bruni, in an editorial in the *New York Times*, wrote, "The [Harvard] report also suggests that colleges discourage manic résumé padding by accepting information on a sharply limited number of extracurricular activities; that they better use essays and references to figure out which students' community-service projects are heartfelt and which are merely window dressing; and that they give full due to the family obligations and part-time work that some underprivileged kids take on." In response to the Harvard report, Yale has already announced that there will be an additional essay on the next iteration of its application that asks applicants "to reflect on engagement with and contribution to their family, community, and/or the public good."

Of course, the reality is that there will always be affluent students who will seek outside help for writing those essays about their "heartfelt community-service projects." Even so, I like to think that this book will offer students, affluent or not, an understanding of how to craft an effective essay and, in so doing, will help level the playing field.

The Supplemental Strategy

Let's say it flat out: the supplementals are a lot of work. Consider the math. If, for instance, you are applying to 20 schools, and each of those schools requires three supplemental essays, that makes for . . . *60 essays?* Are you freaking kidding me?

I can certainly relate to the fear that is engendered by the prospect of having to write 60 essays, especially when that work has to be integrated with schoolwork, extracurricular activities, and such. This is not a time, however, to freak out. It is a time to take a deep breath and apply strategic thinking.

The very first thing you need to do is to pull in all the prompts for all the different essays that are required by all of the schools you are applying to. There is a useful service out there called College Essay Organizer (collegeessayorganizer.com) that will create an essay road map for a fairly nominal fee. You tell them the schools you want to apply to, and they send you back a list of all the essays you will have to write. That way, you get the big picture you need. You can also do all that on your own—it's just a bit more work. In any case, however you decide to do it, you should definitely create that road map so that you can pace yourself and arrive where you ultimately need to get. Once you have all of those prompts in hand, you can formulate a strategy, which begins with categorizing the essays. When you complete that categorizing, you will see that there are certain commonalities that exist from one school's essay requirements to another, and you can begin to develop what I call "template essays." What is a template essay? It is an essay that can easily be adapted from one school to another, with only minor fiddling.

Now it must be understood that some schools have essays that are unique to them. These essays are apt to change from year to year but, for example, in recent years Pomona College has asked students to write this essay:

Pomona's Critical Inquiry course is required of all first-year students, and is designed to be highly interdisciplinary and engaging. Recent class titles include: "The Politics of Classical Art," "Seeing Science," and "The Theatre and Environmental Activism." Imagine you were hired to design and teach a Critical Inquiry course. Describe the title of the class, its contents, and why you chose it.

And then there's this one, from Wake Forest University:

What outrages you and why?

Or how about this one from the University of Richmond:

Tell us about spiders.

These are all examples of essays that do not lend themselves to the template approach. In fact, the last is a good example of the "quirky" essay. Quirky essays are largely designed to display the student's capacity for thinking in new and fresh ways. The student is meant to have fun with these—but also to create an argument that is persuasive, which requires real intellectual rigor.

The University of Chicago is famous for having a long essay (well over five hundred words) that requires the applicant to confront a daunting set of prompts designed by current University of Chicago students. These are totally one-of-a-kind and range from provocative to perplexing to mind-bending. Examples include the following:

- Rerhceseras say it's siltl plisbsoe to raed txet wtih olny the frist and lsat ltteres in palce. This is beaucse the hamun mnid can fnid oderr in dorsdier. Give us your best example of finding order in disorder. (For your reader's sake, please use full sentences with conventional spelling.)
- What's so odd about odd numbers?
- So where is Waldo, really?

These can be fun and are a better place to direct your penchant for quirkiness than in the Common App personal statement. I am not a fan of the quirky personal statement—why I love peanut butter, for example—because I generally feel that they're trying too hard and tend to cloak the writer in quirkiness, rather than revealing the writer's inner life, which is what the personal statement is supposed to be all about. I'm definitely a fan of fun, creative supplemental essays, however, and if you have the motivation to undertake them, then, by all means, go for it. By the same token, if you're a relatively straight shooter and "quirky" feels foreign to you, then you may want to reconsider applying to a school that requires such an essay. Such applications will certainly demand more of your precious time, but there's also the question of whether a school that prizes quirkiness is a good fit for you altogether.

Apart from those unique essays, you will find that most of the supplemental essays fall into these three categories: (1) the academic goals and objectives essay; (2) the extracurricular essay; and (3) the diversity essay. If you can create a "template" essay for each of those, then you will be able to adapt that essay from one school to another, with fairly minor adaptations based on such variables as the specific language of the prompt you're working with and the word count. So let's have a look.

The Academic Goals and Objectives Essay

I have found that the most frequently encountered supplemental essay is the one that asks you to write about your academic goals and objectives. Essentially, this essay asks what you want to study, and why you want to study it at [insert name of college]. This essay lends itself well to a template approach no matter what the word count is or whether the school breaks the essay into two separate, shorter essays ("Why do you want to go to [insert name of college]?" and "What are you interested in studying?").

Let's have a look at how four different schools pose this question:

- **University of Michigan**
  Describe the unique qualities that attract you to the specific College or School (including preferred admission and dual degree programs) to which you are applying. How would that curriculum support your interests? Five-hundred-word limit.

- **Brown University (which splits the academic goals and objectives essay into two essays)**
  Why are you drawn to the area(s) of study you indicated in our Member Section, earlier in this application? If you are "undecided" or not sure which Brown concentrations match your interests, consider describing more generally the academic topics or modes of thought that engage you currently. One-hundred-fifty-word limit.
  Why Brown? Two-hundred-word limit.

- **Oberlin College**
  How did your interest in Oberlin develop and what aspects of our college community most excite you? Two-hundred-fifty-word limit.

- **Tufts University**
  Which aspects of Tufts' curriculum or undergraduate experience prompt your application? In short, "Why Tufts?" Fifty- to one-hundred-word limit.

In creating template essays, I find it easiest to start with the longest length and then cut it down from there. That way, you have the room to form your most complete argument and you can prioritize your points as you face shorter word limits. Although it may seem counterintuitive, I find shorter word limits to be harder to work with than longer limits. No matter the length, however, the content is going to be decidedly similar from one essay to the other.

The way I counsel students to approach the academic goals and objectives essay is to think of it in three parts. The first part explores the genesis of your interest. How did you get interested in engineering? So many students write about LEGO, but that *is* the way for many budding engineers. Or if it is business that you plan to study, how did you get interested in business? Did you set up the proverbial lemonade stand or sell bottled water to joggers? How did you get interested in graphic art? Your mother was a department store buyer, you say, and you and she used to pore over catalogues together? In this first section, you can also talk about such things as early school experiences you had or your experiences being mentored by family or friends who introduced you to certain interests.

The next part of the essay is all about what you have done to advance that interest. High school coursework, independent reading, listening to TED Talks, shadowing professionals, internships, research, jobs, competitions—all of that goes into this section. You have run with your interest and so it has developed nicely.

Those two sections can travel pretty much intact from one school to the other. Yes, you may have to fiddle with your sections to make them fit in certain situations (or, in the case of the Tufts fifty- to one-hundred-word essay, you'll have to adopt a radically different approach, in which you conceive the essay in a new way to accommodate such a meager word allotment). That third part of the essay, however, is customized entirely for the school you're writing for. And this where I tell students to plan on spending time on the Internet, researching the schools that they are applying to.

If you are interested in studying aerospace engineering at the University of Michigan, start off by Googling, "Why study aerospace engineering at University of Michigan?" This will take you to a departmental website that is essentially a selling tool aimed at you, the customer. Like any selling tool, it is built on key marketing messages—and you will want to convey that you have digested those messages by reflecting them back to the school (though not transparently).

You will find key marketing messages on pages like About Us or a Message from the Dean, where you can read about the attributes and values that the school is pushing. Internships? Study abroad? Research? Digest those messages and let the school see that you understand what they are all about. You can cite key courses that strike you as fresh and innovative or mention professors whose work you admire. If you have visited the school and sat in on classes, feel free to write about that and be specific. This means taking notes while you are on your campus visits. Jot down the name of a particularly beautiful quad or building or the name of a professor whose class you sat in on and enjoyed. When it comes time for you to write an essay about why you want to go to Dartmouth or Bowdoin or Georgetown or the University of Rhode Island, you'll be in good shape to talk specifically and not just blather on in generalities about the "rigorous curriculum" and the "distinguished faculty." Yawn.

Also, if the language of the prompt and the space allotment permit, you can cite some nonacademic aspects of the college that appeal to you—anything from sports to community service to arts to location to greenness and so on. Certainly, that would make sense with the "Why Brown?" essay and the Oberlin essay that asks what aspects of the college community most excite you. In short, you need to do your footwork for this part of the essay, which will often lead you to student blogs or student videos that hit some interesting points you can use.

Let's now imagine what an academic goals and objectives essay might look like from a student interested in the intersection of business and technology:

Math has always been my obsession. Where other people see the world in terms of colors, sounds, or kinetics, I think in terms of numbers, seeing sets and patterns. Puzzles have been my partners as far back as I can remember, and when I discovered chess, I immediately focused on the infinite number of randomizations that exist within that game, which is why it became such a passion for me. My true partner and passion, however, is the computer.

My parents bought me my first computer when I was three. The little cartoon duck that taught me simple math quickly became my great ally. Ever since, I have loved playing with computers and trying out new software. In recent years, I have also learned how to remove hardware from my computers and how to install new parts.

To me, computer science is all about problem solving, which I find fascinating and even exhilarating. As a junior, I took AP

Computer Science and totally immersed myself in the process of finding algorithms to solve very complex problems. Currently, I am working on programming a new app to measure body mass index. Drawing upon websites that offer open source software, I find myself spending hours at a time in that state of energized focus and pure enjoyment that Harvard psychologist Mihály Csíkszentmihályi calls "flow." When I am in such a state, I think about what it would be like to spend my life using my computer science expertise in any number of disciplines, from business to polling to scientific research, and I smile.

I am probably most drawn to business. I enjoy people as much as I enjoy computers, and success in business has much to do with understanding how people think and function. As an undergraduate, I would certainly want to develop a strong foundation in the liberal arts, advancing my communications skills and critical thinking. I would also very much enjoy taking psychology courses. With an eye toward entrepreneurship, I would hope to gain insight into my own motivations as well as the motivations of consumers.

When I learned about the Jerome Fisher Program in Management & Technology at UPenn, I felt strongly that I had found the perfect next step for me. This innovative interdisciplinary learning experience explores how the intersection of business and technology can shape our world. Here I would engage in hands-on research with prominent faculty at Penn's Engineering School and find exciting course offerings at Wharton. Management 100 would be a great place to start, providing the opportunity to collaborate on a team with nine other students as we plan and execute a field project for a client in the greater Philadelphia area. Through Wharton, I might also be able to intern with companies like Amazon, Facebook, and Google. Such opportunities would expose me to entirely new ways of thinking about both business and technology. With the knowledge, skills, and insights I would take away from the Jerome Fisher Program, I could go in many different directions, finding paths that I never even knew existed.

I find this essay effective on a number of levels. I get a sense of the writer across the lifeline—from curious child to questing young adult. I also like the fact that he is demonstrating some general knowledge by citing the work of psychologist Csíkszentmihályi. That shows me that this student reads and takes in information. Additionally, I learn that he has a passion for chess, which is nice to know. Somehow, I don't even mind the fact that he refers to his "passions," a word that has become quite overused, because I believe that these are genuine passions, rather than mere lip service to today's buzzword. The writer also makes sensible reference to the value of a liberal arts education, and that is a good note to hit when applying to a liberal arts institution.

As you can see, the writer is following the structure I described previously. The first part of the essay describes the genesis of his interest in computers, with a basis in math. The second part is devoted to how this student advanced that interest (through high school coursework and by working, with open source software, on an app). Everything can stay intact from this school to the next, except for the last paragraph of course. Instead of writing about the Jerome Fisher Program at UPenn, that last paragraph might be devoted to programs at UCLA or Cornell or wherever. The only real work will be to make cuts as called for by the varying word limits.

Now what happens if you have not yet uncovered a strong academic interest and you are undecided? In fact, that is a challenge. Some people think there is a bias against the undecided applicant and, in terms of writing the academic goals and objectives essay, the undecided applicant is looking at a much harder road to travel. However, if you really haven't identified and advanced a strong specific academic interest, then you can't fake it. In such cases, the applicant will have to present his or her situation not as a deficit, but as a strength. For instance, I have had undecided applicants write about being polymaths—i.e., people with wide-ranging knowledge or learning. Such people do exist and some of these applicants have done a very good job of convincing me that they are among this rare breed and they will focus their essays on the value of a broad-based liberal arts education. Other students who are undecided are, in truth, rather unformed, and in those cases the applicant may have to scale down expectations. It's really a case-by-case situation when you're dealing with the undecided applicant.

The Extracurricular Essay

Until fairly recently, there were two required essays on the Common App: the personal statement and a short essay about the applicant's most significant extracurricular activity. When the Common App dropped the latter, many schools picked it up, so it is now one of the more frequently encountered essays. Here is how it looks in three different iterations:

- **Davidson College**
  Please briefly elaborate on one of your extracurricular activities or work experiences. Two-hundred-word limit.

- **Tulane University**
  Please briefly elaborate on one of your extracurricular activities or work experiences. Tw-hundred-fifty-word limit.

- **Bowdoin College**
  Reflecting on your own interests and experiences, please select and respond to one of the following topics:
  (1) Intellectual Engagement; (2) The Common Good;
  (3) Connection to Place. Two-hundred-fifty-word limit.

As you can see, Davidson and Tulane have identical prompts, but with a fifty-word variation on the word limit. Bowdoin, on the other hand, asks students to connect their interests and experiences to one of the three defining qualities that bespeak the Bowdoin undergraduate experience: intellectual engagement, a commitment to the Common Good, and a connection to place. You can address that prompt by pointing your template extracurricular essay toward one of those three defining qualities.

The extracurricular essay rarely goes beyond three hundred words, so let's see what a good one looks like:

Come, oh, songs! Come, oh, dreams!

Soft the gates of day close . . .
There I was, singing Edward MacDowell's "To a Wild Rose" in a recital at Manhattan School of Music. Getting to this moment represented years of hard work and a habit of practice I both cherished and sometimes resented. From the time I was very young, singing has opened up new avenues in my life, providing me with a mode of communication that transcends all barriers. Singing has also given me an enriched sense of community, as I enjoy the companionship of other musicians who pursue their goals with passion and dedication. Do I sometimes wish I did not have this challenge in my life and could bask in leisure? Of course. But notwithstanding the daily practices and the frequent disappointments when I fall short of what I strive for, singing provides me with a unique mix of exhilaration and peace of mind. It is the thing that is most special to me.

Sleep, my birds, sleep, streams!
Sleep, my wild rose!

There are a number of things that I like about this essay. I like the fact that the writer has devoted twenty one out of one hundred seventy three words to the lyrics of the song. To me, this conveys the depth of her interest and her sensitivity to all aspects of the performance. I also like that she alludes to both the pros and the cons of the extracurricular interest. Now let's look at one about chess:

"Check!" I say, as I move my bishop in line with my opponent's king.

My opponent is actually Ted, one of my best friends and certainly my prime chess adversary. Sitting across from me now, holding his head, he knows he cannot escape his fatal position.

Ted and I play chess during our free period almost every day at school. Chess demands creative thinking and strategic vision, which is why we love it. Through chess, we have developed patience and a true and deep capacity for attention. Immersing ourselves in this game, whose ancient roots trace back to Eastern India, has certainly increased our ability to analyze situations and find the best solutions.

"Checkmate," I say—as mildly as I can.

Ted sits there for a moment, resisting the impulse to swipe all the pieces onto the floor with one angry motion, as I have often felt the urge to do.

"Again?" he says.

There is time before the bell rings, at least to start. "Of course," I reply.

Quickly, we set up the board.

Here I like the fact that he has used the chess arena to portray a friendship that feels very real to me. He has thrown in a bit of chess history as well, which leads me to feel that he has a curious mind (always a nice thing for admissions counselors to see). He has also made mention of the strengths that chess has instilled in him—patience, a capacity for attention, the ability to analyze situations—but he hasn't been heavy-handed about it. Most important, note how strong the narrative feeling is in this essay.

The music essay before it also had some narrative touches, and, taken together, these two essays demonstrate how supplemental essays can almost always be invigorated if you approach them as opportunities to tell a story. After all, as we've been saying all along, everyone likes a good story—and no one likes dead-on, routine essays that just sit on the page.

The Diversity Essay

From year to year, I have seen a significant increase in the number of schools that are asking students to write some form of "the diversity essay." This is clearly an invitation to those students from minority backgrounds or unusual educational or family histories to write about themselves. If you're from Greenwich, Connecticut, however, or The Woodlands, Texas, or Marin County, California, then you are living in an environment that is predominantly white and economically advantaged and the diversity essay may leave you scratching your head. Well, so be it. If privileged students have to work a little harder in this instance, then so they shall. In any event, we are indeed living in an increasingly multicultural world and when you get to college, you will likely encounter people from many different cultures that you have not been exposed to before. Thinking and writing about diversity is good preparation for that.

Let's see how three different schools approach this essay:

- **University of Michigan**
  Everyone belongs to many different communities and/or groups defined by (among other things) shared geography, religion, ethnicity, income, cuisine, interest, race, ideology, or intellectual heritage. Choose one of the communities to which you belong, and describe that community and your place within it. Two-hundred-fifty-word limit.

- **Brown University**

  We all exist within communities or groups of various sizes, origins, and purposes; pick one and tell us why it is important to you, and how it has shaped you. One-hundred-fifty-word limit.

- **Duke University**

  Duke University seeks a talented, engaged student body that embodies the wide range of human experience; we believe that the diversity of our students makes our community stronger. If you'd like to share a perspective you bring or experiences you've had to help us understand you better—perhaps related to a community you belong to, your sexual orientation or gender identity, or your family or cultural background—we encourage you to do so. Real people are reading your application, and we want to do our best to understand and appreciate the real people applying to Duke. Two-hundred-fifty-word limit.

For this essay, I have had students write about visiting the Indian temples where their grandparents were married; about eating in an Ethiopian restaurant (and not being Ethiopian); about having a bar mitzvah that focused on cleaning up a roadway; about attending an LGBTQ meeting for the first time; about being an immigrant from Pakistan trying to negotiate the New York subway; and much more. In short, it is an essay that can take the writer in many different directions. It also comes in all different sizes, from the short one-hundred-fifty-word essay that Brown asks for to a five-hundred-word version that Rice University required a few years ago. Let's see how one student approached that Brown essay, whose prompt was as follows: "We all exist within communities or groups of various sizes, origins, and purposes; pick one and tell us why it is important to you, and how it has shaped you."

"Careful, Lizzie."

I looked around to see Homer, my boss, watching as I wrestled with a crate of eggplants. I had been working here at the farmers' market every Saturday morning for more than a year, volunteering with Helpful Hands, a community-supported agricultural cooperative that provides people with local produce farmed sustainably.

I had grown up with little attention paid to things like organic eggplants. My parents had been raised on Twinkies and Perdue, but at least they were willing to learn. When I began working in my school's organic garden, I brought valuable lessons home and soon we were all happy vegetarians. Taking it to the next level, I got involved with Helping Hands, a community that connects me to people I would never have known otherwise.

"I'm good, Homer," I said, remembering to lift with my knees.

I love these Saturday mornings and will miss them next year.

Again, note the small narrative hook at the beginning. See how engaging it is to start an essay that way? I always tell students that one of the reasons why people enjoy reading is because it takes them to places they have never been. So if a student can show me what it's like to walk a tightrope, fly in a hot air balloon, watch a bullfight, eat twenty hot dogs in one sitting, be bitten by a parrot, or work at a farmers' market—all things I have never experienced—then I'm with that writer from the get-go.

Now, to see what another version of the diversity essay looks like, consider this one by a student writing to the two-hundred-fifty-word Duke limit. It's also a good example of what you can write if you hail from a small town that lacks real diversity.

"Mars Bar, Carter?" said Jamie, my partner for the night.

I was a diehard Snickers guy myself, but wasn't going to turn him down. It had been a rough six hours anyway. Two calls when many nights we don't get any. One was easy enough—a man with a back spasm—but the second, from an old lady in congestive heart failure, was far from easy.

"Sure," I said. "Hand it over."

The rescue squad in my small town in Virginia is a magnet for all kinds of people. We have two retired teachers, a gay machinist, a piano tuner, a woman plumber, some kids who aren't going anywhere in the very near future, and a few, like me, with their eye on a college education. We all get along, however, because we share a common purpose: to help people in need.

Working on the rescue squad has taught me not to have preconceptions about my neighbors. It's also taught me that you can learn a lot from people you might not otherwise have paid much attention to. People like Jamie, who's 44 years old, served in Iraq, and makes his living as a roofer, give you a whole new perspective on the world. It pays to keep your eyes, ears, and mind open.

"Can't wait to get into bed tonight," I said, finishing off the Mars Bar.

"Don't I know it," said Jamie, as we drove through the dark, cold night.

Now there's an essay that shows how diversity exists within every community. It's just a matter of locating it. And diversity does not have to be about race, gender, or ethnicity only. Economic diversity can be a very powerful thing to write about. This essay also demonstrates, once again, the power of the narrative. Constructing your essay with an idea of the elements of the narrative that we have been talking about all along—"The Once," The Point, etc.—will confer a power on your piece that would not be there if you just told us in the usual, run-of-the-mill fashion about how, "Being in the rescue squad has taught me so much and has helped me develop my facilities of interpersonal communication, problem solving, and yadda yadda."

It's a *story*, people—which is what we like to read.

The Short-Short on Short-Shorts

Some schools, like Yale, Stanford, and Columbia, ask you to write very short responses to a series of questions. There are potential traps in these questions as well. For instance, Yale asks you to list the books you read for pleasure last year. Are there any wrong answers? Maybe. I counseled one student about citing *The Fountainhead* by Ayn Rand, as some folks in academia regard Rand as a kind of crypto-Fascist. So why risk it? Similarly, Stanford asks you to name your favorite books, authors, films, and artists. I've had students include *The Hunger Games* and the *Harry Potter* series, which you may love and which are perfectly fine to love, but these can be seen by some snobbish admissions counselors as low-end, so again, why risk it? Stanford also asks you to list five words that best describe you. I advise students to stay away from "happy," "cheerful," "polite," "ambitious," "literal," and quite a few other descriptors I've seen. How do you know if your descriptor is a good one or not? Hard to say. You have to be very attuned to the nuance of words. So "happy," "cheerful," and "polite" can sound insipid to some hardened ears, while "ambitious" can sound shark-like to softer ears. "Literal" is just plain confusing. Did you mean "literary"? On the other hand, words like "purposeful," "organized," "responsible," "determined," "considerate," and "thoughtful" are all reasonably good descriptors and there are hundreds more to choose from.

Generally speaking, a misstep on these short-shorts can bring down the overall level of your application, so it's best to take these quite seriously, show your answers around to your trusted advisors, absorb their advice, and make your changes accordingly.

Wait . . . Wait . . .

We haven't finished yet. We still want to discuss the wait list letter, should you find yourself suspended in that particular limbo. Many students in that situation feel compelled to write something—*anything*—to the admissions committee, but, as with most things in life, there is a right way and a wrong way to proceed.

First of all, it's important to note that you will not be writing an essay in this situation but, rather, a letter. It is a letter that is intended to continue to interest the admissions committee in you and your application. First make sure, however, that this is a school that is open to hearing from you. Your college counselor may be able to let you know that or you can try to find out on the Internet. If, in fact, they are open to it, then send them a letter that accomplishes the following:

1. *Express your appreciation and your interest.* Let the admissions committee know that you thank them for letting you get this far and that you would like to go even further.

2. *Reaffirm why _____ is the right school for you.* Be specific and cite interesting news or developments at the school. If you're applying in biomedical engineering, for instance, pore over their biomedical engineering departmental website, gather up whatever big news is cited there, and mention it as all the more reason why you want to go. It makes you look informed and it impresses them with your diligence.

3. *Inform them about current distinctions.* Are you going to be the valedictorian or salutatorian? Let them know that. Have you achieved some special recognition in your field of interest, whether it's scientific research, the violin, soccer, or community service? Be sure to let them know that as well.

All in all, this is not the easiest letter in the world to write, but the saving grace is that you can and should keep it to one side of a page. Brevity is key in this instance. Note too that you must never sound pleading in this letter. Locutions such as, "I would do anything to be part of the class of 2020" are deadly.

Here is a letter from a student who was wait-listed at Harvard that serves as a good model for this sort of thing. Unfortunately, it didn't gain its writer a place in the in-coming Harvard class, as few people turn this place down, but we can still learn from it.

Dear_____(note: It's nice if you can actually address this to a real person)

I regard it as a great honor to have earned a place on the Harvard wait list and wish to reaffirm my interest in becoming part of the Harvard community.

Several recent developments in Harvard's Department of Government further convince me that this would be the ideal setting for my undergraduate education. I was fascinated to read about "The Global Philosopher," Professor Michael Sandel's new program on the BBC about immigration and the ethics of national borders. This seems so timely in the face of our national discussion of these issues in this election year. I was also interested to see that Professor Stephen Ansolabahere's book *Cheap and Clean: How Americans Think About Energy in the Age of Global Warming* was selected as the recipient of the 2015 Don K. Price Award, which recognizes the best book on Science, Technology, and Environmental Politics published in the last year. Environmental politics is a strong interest of mine and I would very much appreciate the chance to study with Professor Ansolabahere.

I am pleased to report that there have been several note-worthy developments in my life as well since I applied last fall. I have been chosen by the National Merit Scholarship Corporation to be one of 2500 students who will receive a $2500 National Merit Scholarship. Also, as a lifelong member of the Girl Scouts, I was thrilled to be one of only 5.4 percent of members nationally to receive the coveted Gold Award. This was in recognition of my project to help restore Sunny Side Park in my hometown of Lewiston, Maine. I recruited and led a team to make this a safer and more enjoyable place for Lewiston residents, rebuilding picnic tables, weeding gardens, and adding new plantings.

I would be happy to provide you with any further information that you might want to know and could visit campus or participate in any additional interviews as necessary. Again, I appreciate your consideration.

Sincerely,
Diana Leventhal

In short, you will want to keep such a letter brief, relevant, and unadorned. And, also, keep this in mind: if you do not gain acceptance to a school that has wait-listed you or to any of your reach schools, you can still do just fine at the school where you do matriculate. As someone who has written a great deal of recruitment and development materials for a wide range of schools, I have seen extraordinary students at lesser-known institutions. With the right work ethic, good study habits, a desire to learn, and the ability to find and make use of mentors, there should be no ceiling on any student's success.

APPENDIX 3: FOR PARENTS

I have discovered that as many parents as students read my book, so why not a section for you guys?

Naturally, as a college essay coach, I interface a great deal with parents. Almost always, I regard them as allies and they act as allies. When a student goes AWOL, I enlist them to track that kid down. Also, sometimes a parent will mention something to me about a child and it will actually become the source material for a very good essay. Then there are times when parents question our product and feel that something is not quite there—some aspect of their child that should be more present in the essay—and I listen carefully and sometimes agree that the parent is right and we go back to the drawing board. Occasionally, I have to deal with a parent who is a bit overwrought about the whole admissions process—and why wouldn't you be? It's just a tad stressful, no? And then I will gently suggest that the parent back off and give us a little room to work. Almost all the parents I've had contact with have been able to do that, I'm pleased to say.

So what can a parent do to help with this business of writing a college admissions essay? Let me mention a few things:

1. Help your child get organized. These days, the amount of writing that actually goes into a college application can be overwhelming. Parents should try not to get into conflicts

with their kids around all of this, but, instead, really try to see themselves as agents of support who are there expressly to meet the needs of their kids. This is a time for nurturing.

2. Provide snacks. Raw carrots and celery sticks, peanut butter on rice crackers—they need the foods from their toddlerhood, because there is going to be a lot of regression.

3. Offer positive reinforcement. If your son or daughter shows you a draft of what he or she has written (which I hope won't happen; much better for that to wait until the piece is finished), find something good to say about it. This early drafting stage is the time for positives, not negatives.

4. Do not offer advice about things you don't know about. Please don't tell your child that he or she can't write about grandparents, pets, sports injuries, or any of the stuff that somebody might have told you is off limits. As you've seen in this book, nothing is off limits. There are no new stories. There are only new and interesting ways to tell them, and that is your child's task—to find an interesting, new way to tell a story. If he or she finds that, then that pet story will come alive and will be absolutely as good an essay as anything else.

5. Do not, under any circumstances, try to write the essay for your child. First of all, it's unethical—and a lack of ethics is not a good thing for parents to model. Second, you won't do a good job trying to sound like your child. You're not seventeen. Third, if your son or daughter cannot get it together to finish the college application process, then he or she may not be ready to go away to school. And that's the truth.

Good luck, parents. It's not an easy job, but somebody has to do it.

APPENDIX 4: NEW FOR TEACHERS

Conquering the College Admissions Essay in 10 Steps is an ideal classroom resource because it's all about writing. Now we are offering a free teacher's guide, available for download at www.conquerthecollegeessay.com/teachersguide.

The guide is designed with several outcomes in mind. First and foremost, students will compose a polished personal statement. Through the process of writing and revising, they'll also come to a better understanding of themselves as writers. Finally, they'll receive vital practice in reading and using informational text. Each of the ten lesson plans includes:

- a brief overview of the lesson
- an estimate of the time needed
- Common Core Standards covered
- step-by-step instructions
- a materials list
- post-lesson evaluation questions

A set of handout masters directly follows the lesson plans.

The guide was developed and prepared by Katie Doolittle, who holds a bachelor's degree from Brown University and a master's degree in teaching from Seattle University. Katie is National Board–certified in the area of adolescent and young adult English language arts. Over the course of seven years working at the high school level, she has taught classes ranging from reading remediation to advanced placement language and composition.

Please also note that Alan Gelb always likes to hear from teachers with any questions or thoughts they have about his book, the guide, or the college admissions essay in general.

You can reach him at alan@conquerthecollegeessay.com.

ABOUT THE AUTHOR

Alan Gelb is a college essay coach and professional writer whose clients include colleges and universities across the country. He is the author of *The Complete Student: Achieving Success in College and Beyond* and *Having the Last Say: Capturing Your Legacy in One Small Story*, among others. Alan lives with his family in East Chatham, New York.

Visit www.conquerthecollegeessay.com for more information.

Index

MORE COLLEGE GUIDANCE FROM TEN SPEED PRESS

COLLEGE RULES!, 4TH EDITION
How to Study, Survive,
and Succeed in College
Sherrie Nist-Olejnik and Jodi
Patrick Holschuh
$14.99 (Canada: $19.99)
ISBN: 978-1-60774-852-6
eBook ISBN: 978-0-60774-853-3

**10 THINGS EMPLOYERS WANT YOU
TO LEARN IN COLLEGE, REVISED**
The Skills You Need to Succeed
Bill Coplin
$14.99 (Canada: $17.99)
ISBN: 978-1-60774-145-9
eBook ISBN: 978-0-307-76849-0

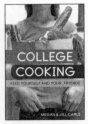

COLLEGE COOKING
Feed Yourself and Your Friends
Megan Carle and Jill Carle
$19.99 (Canada: $24.99)
ISBN: 978-1-58008-826-8
eBook ISBN: 978-1-60774-121-3

**WHAT COLOR IS YOUR PARACHUTE?
FOR TEENS, THIRD EDITION**
Discover Yourself, Design Your
Future, and Plan for Your Dream Job
Carol Christen and Richard N. Bolles
$15.99 (Canada: $18.99)
ISBN: 978-1-60774-577-8
eBook ISBN: 978-1-60774-578-5

TEN SPEED PRESS
California | New York